Praise for *Implementation Patterns*

"Kent is a master at creating code that communicates well, is easy to understand, and is a pleasure to read. Every chapter of this book contains excellent explanations and insights into the smaller but important decisions we continuously have to make when creating quality code and classes."
—*Erich Gamma, IBM Distinguished Engineer*

"Many teams have a master developer who makes a rapid stream of good decisions all day long. Their code is easy to understand, quick to modify, and feels safe and comfortable to work with. If you ask how they thought to write something the way they did, they always have a good reason. This book will help you become the master developer on your team. The breadth and depth of topics will engage veteran programmers, who will pick up new tricks and improve on old habits, while the clarity makes it accessible to even novice developers."
—*Russ Rufer, Silicon Valley Patterns Group*

"Many people don't realize how readable code can be and how valuable that readability is. Kent has taught me so much, I'm glad this book gives everyone the chance to learn from him."
—*Martin Fowler, chief scientist, ThoughtWorks*

"Code should be worth reading, not just by the compiler, but by humans. Kent Beck distilled his experience into a cohesive collection of implementation patterns. These nuggets of advice will make your code truly worth reading."
—*Gregor Hohpe, author of* Enterprise Integration Patterns

"In this book Kent Beck shows how writing clear and readable code follows from the application of simple principles. *Implementation Patterns* will help developers write intention revealing code that is both easy to understand and flexible towards future extensions. A must read for developers who are serious about their code."
—*Sven Gorts*

"*Implementation Patterns* bridges the gap between design and coding. Beck introduces a new way of thinking about programming by basing his discussion on values and principles."
—*Diomidis Spinellis, author of* Code Reading *and* Code Quality

Implementation Patterns

The Addison-Wesley Signature Series

The Addison-Wesley Signature Series provides readers with practical and authoritative information on the latest trends in modern technology for computer professionals. The series is based on one simple premise: great books come from great authors. Books in the series are personally chosen by expert advisors, world-class authors in their own right. These experts are proud to put their signatures on the covers, and their signatures ensure that these thought leaders have worked closely with authors to define topic coverage, book scope, critical content, and overall uniqueness. The expert signatures also symbolize a promise to our readers: you are reading a future classic.

THE ADDISON–WESLEY SIGNATURE SERIES
SIGNERS: KENT BECK AND MARTIN FOWLER

Kent Beck has pioneered people-oriented technologies like JUnit, Extreme Programming, and patterns for software development. Kent is interested in helping teams do well by doing good — finding a style of software development that simultaneously satisfies economic, aesthetic, emotional, and practical constraints. His books focus on touching the lives of the creators and users of software.

Martin Fowler has been a pioneer of object technology in enterprise applications. His central concern is how to design software well. He focuses on getting to the heart of how to build enterprise software that will last well into the future. He is interested in looking behind the specifics of technologies to the patterns, practices, and principles that last for many years; these books should be usable a decade from now. Martin's criterion is that these are books he wished he could write.

TITLES IN THE SERIES

Implementation Patterns
Kent Beck, ISBN 0321413091

Test-Driven Development: By Example
Kent Beck, ISBN 0321146530

User Stories Applied: For Agile Software Development
Mike Cohn, ISBN 0321205685

Implementing Lean Software Development: From Concept to Cash
Mary and Tom Poppendieck, ISBN 0321437381

Refactoring Databases: Evolutionary Database Design
Scott W. Ambler and Pramodkumar J. Sadalage, ISBN 0321293533

Continuous Integration: Improving Software Quality and Reducing Risk
Paul M. Duvall, with Steve Matyas and Andrew Glover, 0321336380

Patterns of Enterprise Application Architecture
Martin Fowler, ISBN 0321127420

Beyond Software Architecture: Creating and Sustaining Winning Solutions
Luke Hohmann, ISBN 0201775948

Enterprise Integration Patterns: Designing, Building, and Deploying Messaging Solutions
Gregor Hohpe and Bobby Woolf, ISBN 0321200683

Refactoring to Patterns
Joshua Kerievsky, ISBN 0321213351

xUnit Test Patterns: Refactoring Test Code
Gerard Meszaros, 0131495054

Implementation Patterns

Kent Beck

⋏ Addison-Wesley

Upper Saddle River, NJ • Boston • Indianapolis • San Francisco
New York • Toronto • Montreal • London • Munich • Paris • Madrid
Cape Town • Sydney • Tokyo • Singapore • Mexico City

Many of the designations used by manufacturers and sellers to distinguish their products are claimed as trademarks. Where those designations appear in this book, and the publisher was aware of a trademark claim, the designations have been printed with initial capital letters or in all capitals.

The author and publisher have taken care in the preparation of this book, but make no expressed or implied warranty of any kind and assume no responsibility for errors or omissions. No liability is assumed for incidental or consequential damages in connection with or arising out of the use of the information or programs contained herein.

The publisher offers excellent discounts on this book when ordered in quantity for bulk purchases or special sales, which may include electronic versions and/or custom covers and content particular to your business, training goals, marketing focus, and branding interests. For more information, please contact:

U.S. Corporate and Government Sales
(800) 382-3419
corpsales@pearsontechgroup.com

For sales outside the United States please contact:

International Sales
international@pearsoned.com

This Book Is Safari Enabled

The Safari® Enabled icon on the cover of your favorite technology book means the book is available through Safari Bookshelf. When you buy this book, you get free access to the online edition for 45 days.

Safari Bookshelf is an electronic reference library that lets you easily search thousands of technical books, find code samples, download chapters, and access technical information whenever and wherever you need it.

To gain 45-day Safari Enabled access to this book:

• Go to http://www.awprofessional.com/safarienabled

• Complete the brief registration form

• Enter the coupon code LBKN-XFGJ-AKJW-IUJ3-9H3D

If you have difficulty registering on Safari Bookshelf or accessing the online edition, please e-mail customer-service@safaribooksonline.com.

Visit us on the Web: www.awprofessional.com

Library of Congress Cataloging-in-Publication Data

Beck, Kent.

  Implementation patterns / Kent Beck.

    p. cm.

  Includes bibliographical references and index.

  ISBN-13: 978-0-321-41309-3 (pbk. : alk. paper)

  1. Software patterns. 2. Computer software--Development. I. Title.

  QA76.76.P37B33 2007

  005.1--dc22

                                        2007035166

ISBN-13: 978-0-321-41309-3

ISBN 0-321-41309-1

Text printed in the United States on recycled paper at Courier in Westford, Massachusetts.

2nd Printing   December 2007

To Cindee: Thank you for your encouragement, insistence, food, soothing, irritation, editing, and tea. The dedication of a book is as a raisin to an elephant compared to what you give me.
Bless you.

Contents

Preface

This is a book about programming—specifically, about programming so other people can understand your code. There is no magic to writing code other people can read. It's like all writing—know your audience, have a clear overall structure in mind, express the details so they contribute to the whole story. Java offers some good ways to communicate. The implementation patterns here are Java programming habits that result in readable code.

Another way to look at implementation patterns is as a way of thinking "What do I want to tell a reader about this code?" Programmers spend so much of their time in their own heads that trying to look at the world from someone else's viewpoint is a big shift. Not just "What will the computer do with this code?" but "How can I communicate what I am thinking to people?" This shift in perspective is healthy and potentially profitable, since so much software development money is spent on understanding existing code.

There is an American game show called Jeopardy in which the host supplies answers and the contestants try to guess the questions. "A word describing being thrown through a window." "What is 'defenestration'?" "Correct."

Coding is like Jeopardy. Java provides answers in the form of its basic constructs. Programmers usually have to figure out for themselves what the questions are, what problems are solved by each language construct. If the answer is "Declare a field as a Set." the question might be "How can I tell other programmers that a collection contains no duplicates?" The implementation patterns provide a catalog of the common problems in programming and the features of Java that address those problems.

Scope management is as important in book writing as it is in software development. Here are some things this book is not. It is not a style guide because it contains too much explanation and leaves the final decisions up to the reader. It is not a design book because it is mostly concerned with smaller-scale decisions, the kind programmers make many times a day. It's not a patterns book because the format of the patterns is idiosyncratic and *ad hoc* (literally "built for a particular purpose"). It's not a language book because, while it covers many Java language features, it assumes readers already know Java.

Actually this book is built on a rather fragile premise: that good code matters. I have seen too much ugly code make too much money to believe that quality of code is either necessary or sufficient for commercial success or widespread use. However, I still believe that quality of code matters even if it doesn't provide control over the future. Businesses that are able to develop and release with confidence, shift direction in response to opportunities and competition, and maintain positive morale through challenges and setbacks will tend to be more successful than businesses with shoddy, buggy code.

Even if there was no long-term economic impact from careful coding I would still choose to write the best code I could. A seventy-year lifespan contains just over two billion seconds. That's not enough seconds to waste on work I'm not proud of. Coding well is satisfying, both the act itself and the knowledge that others will be able to understand, appreciate, use, and extend my work.

In the end, then, this is a book about responsibility. As a programmer you have been given time, talent, money, and opportunity. What will you do to make responsible use of these gifts? The pages that follow contain my answer to this question for me: code for others as well as myself and my buddy the CPU.

Acknowledgments

First, last, and always I would like to thank Cynthia Andres, my partner, editor, support, and chief butt-kicker. My friend Paul Petralia got this project going with me and provided encouraging phone calls throughout. My editor Chris Guzikowski and I learned how to work together over the course of this project. He gave me the support I needed from the Pearson side to finish the book. Thank you to the production team at Pearson: Julie Nahil, John Fuller, and Cynthia Kogut. Jennifer Kohnke produced illustrations that combine information and humanity. My reviewers provided clear, timely feedback for my drafts: Erich Gamma, Steve Metsker, Diomidis Spinellis, Tom deMarco, Michael Feathers, Doug Lea, Brad Abrams, Cliff Click, Pekka Abrahamson, Gregor Hohpe and Michele Marchesi. Thank you to David Saff for recognizing the symmetry between state and behavior. My children who remain at home kept reminding me of why I wanted to be finished: Lincoln, Lindsey, Forrest, and Joëlle Andres-Beck.

Chapter 1

Introduction

Here we are together. You've picked up my book (it's yours now). You already write code. You have probably already developed a style of your own through your own experiences.

The goal of this book is to help you communicate your intentions through your code. The book begins with an overview of programming and patterns (chapters 2-4). The remainder of the book (chapters 5-8) is a series of short essays, patterns, on how to use the features of Java to write readable code. It closes with a chapter on how to modify the advice here if you are writing frameworks instead of applications. Throughout, the book is focused on programming techniques that enhance communication.

There are several steps to communicating through code. First I had to become conscious while programming. I had been programming for years when I first started writing implementation patterns. I was astonished to discover that, even though programming decisions came smoothly and quickly to me, I couldn't explain why I was so sure a method should be called such-and-so or that a bit of logic belonged in this object over here. The first step towards communicating was slowing down long enough to become aware of what I was thinking, to stop pretending that I coded by instinct.

The second step was acknowledging the importance of other people. I found programming satisfying, but I am self-centered. Before I could write communicative code I needed to believe that other people were as important as I was. Programming is hardly ever a solitary communion between one man and one machine. Caring about other people is a conscious decision, and one that requires practice.

Which brings me to the third step. Once I had exposed my thinking to sunlight and fresh air and acknowledged that other people had as much right to exist as I did, I needed to demonstrate my new perspective in practice. I use the implementation patterns here to program consciously and for others as well as myself.

You can read this book strictly for technical content—useful tricks with explanations. However, I thought it fair to warn you that there is a whole lot more going on, at least for me.

You can find those technical bits by thumbing through the patterns chapters. One effective strategy for learning this material is to read it just before you need to use it. To read it "just-in-time", I suggest skipping right to chapter 5 and skimming through to the end, then keeping the book by you as you program. After you've used many of the patterns, you can come back to the introductory material for the philosophical background behind the ideas you've been using.

If you are interested in a thorough understanding of the material here, you can read straight through from the beginning. Unlike most of my books, however, the chapters here are quite long, so it will take concentration on your part to read end-to-end.

Most of the material in this book is organized as patterns. Most decisions in programming are similar to decisions that have come before. You might name a million variables in your programming career. You don't come up with a completely novel approach to naming each variable. The general constraints on naming are always the same: you need to convey the purpose, type, and lifetime of the variable to readers, you need to pick a name that's easy to read, you need to pick a name that's easy to write and format. Add to these general constraints the specifics of a particular variable and you come up with a workable name. Naming variables is an example of a pattern: the decision and its constraints repeat even though you might create a different name each time.

I think patterns often need different presentations. Sometimes an argumentative essay best explains a pattern, sometimes a diagram, sometimes a teaching story, sometimes an example. Rather than cram each pattern's description into a rigid format, I have described each in the way I thought best.

This book contains 77 explicitly named patterns, each covering some aspect of writing readable code. In addition, there are many smaller patterns or variants of patterns that I mention in passing. My goal with this book is to offer advice for how to approach most common, daily coding tasks so as to help future readers understand what the code is supposed to do.

This book fits somewhere between *Design Patterns* and a Java language manual. *Design Patterns* talks about decisions you might make a few times a day while developing, typically decisions that regulate the interaction between objects. You apply an implementation pattern every few seconds while programming. While language manuals are good at describing what you can do with Java, they don't talk much about why you would use a certain construct or what someone reading your code is likely to conclude from it.

Part of my philosophy in writing this book has been to stick to topics I know well. Concurrency issues, for example, are not addressed in these implementation patterns, not because concurrency isn't an important issue, but rather because it is not one on which I have a lot to say. My concurrency strategy has always been to isolate as much as possible concurrent parts of my applications. While I am generally successful in doing so, it's not something I can explain. I recommend a book such as *Java Concurrency in Practice* for a practical look at concurrency.

Another topic not addressed in this book is any notion of software process. The advice about communicating through code here is intended to work whether that code is written near the end of a long cycle or seconds after a failing test has been written. Software that costs less overall is good to have, whatever the sociological trappings within which it is written.

I also stop short of the edges of Java. I tend to be conservative in my technology choices because I have been burned too often pushing new features to their limits (it's a fine learning strategy but too risky for most development). So, you'll find here a pedestrian subset of Java. If you are motivated to use the latest features of Java, you can learn them from other sources.

Tour Guide

The book is divided into seven major sections as seen in Figure 1.1. Here they are:

- Introduction—these short chapters describe the importance and value of communicating through code and the philosophy behind patterns.

- Class—patterns describing how and why you might create classes and how classes encode logic.

- State—patterns for storing and retrieving state.

- Behavior—patterns for representing logic, especially alternative paths.

- Method—patterns for writing methods, reminding you what readers are likely to conclude from your choice of method decomposition and names.

- Collections—patterns for choosing and using collections.

- Evolving Frameworks—variations on the preceding patterns when building frameworks instead of applications.

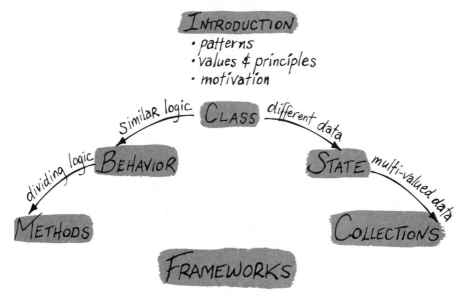

Figure 1.1 *Book overview*

And Now...

...to the meat of the book. If you are reading straight through, just turn the page (I suppose you would have figured that one out for yourself). If you want to browse the patterns themselves, start with chapter 5, page 21. Happy implementing.

Chapter 2

Patterns

Many decisions in programming are unique. How you approach programming a web site will be quite different from how you approach building a pacemaker. However, as the decisions become more and more purely technical, a sense of familiarity sets in. Didn't I just write this code? Programming would be more effective if programmers spent less time on the mundane, repetitive parts of their job so they had more time to spend doing a good job of solving truly unique problems.

Most programs follow a small set of laws:

- Programs are read more often than they are written.

- There is no such thing as "done". Much more investment will be spent modifying programs than developing them initially.

- They are structured using a basic set of state and control flow concepts.

- Readers need to understand programs in detail and in concept. Sometimes they move from detail to concept, sometimes from concept to detail.

Patterns are based on this commonality. For example, every programmer has to decide how to structure iteration. By the time you are thinking about how to write a loop, most of the domain-specific questions have been resolved for the moment and you are left with purely technical issues: the loop should be easy to read, easy to write, easy to verify, easy to modify, and efficient.

This list of concerns is the beginning of a pattern. The constraints or *forces* listed above affect how every loop in a program is written. The forces recur predictably, which is one sense in which a pattern is a pattern: it is a pattern of forces.

There are a few reasonable ways to write a loop. Each of them implies different priorities between the constraints. If performance is more important you might structure the loop one way, while if ease of modification is more important you might structure it differently.

Each pattern illustrates a point of view about the relative priorities of the forces. Most patterns come with a little essay about the alternatives for solving the problem and why the recommended solution is superior. Revealing the reasoning behind the advice in a pattern invites readers to decide for themselves how they want to approach a recurring problem.

As hinted above, each pattern also comes with the seed of a solution. The pattern for loops over a collection might suggest, "Use the Java5 for loop to express iteration." Patterns bridge from abstract principles to practice. Patterns help you write code.

Patterns work together. The pattern suggesting a for loop introduces the problem of what to name the loop variable. Rather than pack everything into a single pattern, there is another pattern specifically covering variable naming.

The style of presentation for the patterns varies considerably in this book. Sometimes patterns are clearly named, with sections to discuss the forces and solution. Some of the smaller patterns, though, are embedded within a larger pattern. A sentence or two may be all the discussion a little pattern needs.

Working with patterns can feel constraining at times but using a pattern can save time and energy. For example, making a bed takes much less energy to do by habit than if you had to think out each step in the process and work out the correct order each time. You have a set pattern for bed-making which greatly simplifies that chore. If the bed is against the wall or the sheet is too small you adapt your strategy to the situation, but overall bed-making can be done by rote, freeing your mind for more interesting and unique tasks. As a pattern becomes habit I find I appreciate not having to raise a debate just to write a loop. If the whole team becomes dissatisfied with a pattern, they can discuss their options for introducing a new pattern.

No one set of patterns will work in all programming situations. Listed later in this book are the patterns that I use and that I have observed to work well in application development (with a brief foray into framework development). Blindly copying anyone's style is not as effective as thinking about and practicing your own style and discussing and sharing a style within your team.

Patterns work best as aids to human decision making. Some of the implementation patterns will eventually make their way into programming languages just as structured uses of setjmp()/longjmp() became today's exception handling system. In the meantime, patterns often require adaptation before they are used.

This chapter opened with the search for a cheaper, quicker, less energy-consuming way to solve the common problems in programming. Using patterns helps programmers write reasonable solutions to common problems, leaving more time, energy, and creativity to apply to the truly unique problems. Each pattern bundles a common problem of programming with a discussion of the factors affecting that problem and provides concrete advice about how to quickly create a satisfactory solution. The result is a better/cheaper/faster job on the boring parts of programs and more time and energy to invest in the unique problems of each program.

The following chapter, "A Theory of Programming", describes the values and principles underlying the style of programming described by these implementation patterns.

Chapter 3

A Theory of Programming

No list of patterns, no matter how exhaustive, can cover every situation that comes up while programming. Eventually (or even frequently) you'll come upon a situation where none of the cookie cutters fits. This need for general approaches to unique problems is one reason to study the theory of programming. Another is the sense of mastery that comes of knowing both what to do and why. Conversations about programming are also more interesting when they cover both theory and practice.

Each pattern carries with it a little bit of theory. There are larger and more pervasive forces at work in programming than are covered in individual patterns, however. This section describes these cross-cutting concerns. They are divided here into two types: values and principles. The values are the universal overarching themes of programming. When I am working well, I hold dear the importance of communicating with other people, removing excess complexity from my code, and keeping my options open. These values—communication, simplicity, and flexibility—color every decision I make while programming.

The principles described here aren't as far-reaching or pervasive as the values, but each one is expressed by many of the patterns. The principles bridge between the values, which are universal but often difficult to apply directly, and the patterns, which are clear to apply but specific. I have found it valuable to make the principles explicit for those situations where no pattern applies, or when two mutually exclusive patterns apply equally. Faced with ambiguity, understanding the principles allows me to "make something up" that is consistent with the rest of my practice and likely to turn out well.

These three elements—values, principles, and patterns—form a balanced expression of a style of development. The patterns describe what to do. The values provide motivation. The principles help translate motive into action.

The values, principles, and patterns here are drawn from my own practice, reflection, and conversation with other programmers. We all draw from the experience of previous generations of programmers. The result is *a* style of development, not *the* style of development. Different values and different principles will lead to different styles. One of the advantages of laying out a programming style as values, principles, and practices is that it is easier to have productive conflict about programming this way. If you want to do something one way and I another, we can identify the level of our disagreement and avoid wasting time. If we disagree about principles, arguing about where curly braces belong won't solve the underlying discord.

Values

Three values that are consistent with excellence in programming are communication, simplicity, and flexibility. While these three sometimes conflict, more often they complement each other. The best programs offer many options for future extension, contain no extraneous elements, and are easy to read and understand.

Communication

Code communicates well when a reader can understand it, modify it, or use it. While programming it's tempting to think only of the computer. However, good things happen when I think of others while I program. I get cleaner code that is easier to read, it is more cost-effective, my thinking is clearer, I give myself a fresh perspective, my stress level drops, and I meet some of my social needs. Part of what drew me to programming in the first place was the opportunity to commune with something outside myself. However, I didn't want to deal with sticky, inexplicable, annoying human beings. Programming as if people didn't really exist paled after only a couple of decades. Building ever-more-elaborate sugar castles in my mind became colorless and stale.

One of the early experiences that led me to focus on communication was discovering Knuth's *Literate Programming*: a progam should read like a book. It should have plot, rhythm, and delightful little turns of phrase.

When Ward Cunningham and I first read about literate programs, we decided to try it. We sat down with one of the cleanest pieces of code in the Smalltalk image, the ScrollController, and tried to make it into a story. Hours later we had completely rewritten the code on our way to a reasonable paper. Every time a bit of logic was a little hard to explain, it was easier to rewrite the code than explain why the code was hard to understand. The demands of communication changed our perspective on coding.

There is a sound economic basis for focusing on communication while programming. The majority of the cost of software is incurred after the software has been first deployed. Thinking about my experience of modifying code, I see that I spend much more time reading the existing code than I do writing new code. If I want to make my code cheap, therefore, I should make it easy to read.

Focusing on communication improves thinking by being more realistic. Part of the improvement comes from engaging more of my brain. When I think, "How would someone else see this?" different neurons are firing than when I'm just focused on myself and my computer. I take a step back from my isolated perspective and see my problem and solution anew. Another part of the improvement comes from the reduced stress of knowing that I am taking care of business, doing the right thing. Finally, as a socially oriented species, explicitly accounting for social issues is more realistic than working at pretending they don't exist.

Simplicity

In *The Visual Display of Quantitative Information*, Edward Tufte has an exercise where he takes a graph and starts erasing all the marks that don't add information. The resulting graph is novel and much easier to understand than the original.

Eliminating excess complexity enables those reading, using, and modifying programs to understand them more quickly. Some of the complexity is essential, accurately reflecting the complexity of the problem to be solved. Some of the complexity, though, represents the claw marks our fingernails make as we struggle to get the program to run at all. It is this excess complexity that removes value from software, both by making the software less likely to run correctly and more difficult to change successfully in the future. Part of programming is to look back at what you've done and separate the wheat from the chaff.

Simplicity is in the eye of the beholder. What is simple to an expert programmer, familiar with the power tools of the craft, might be overwhelmingly complex to a beginner. Just as good prose is written with an audience in mind, so good programs are written with an audience in mind. Challenging your audience a little is fine, but too much complexity will lose them.

Computing advances in waves of complexity and simplification. Mainframe architectures became more and more baroque until mini-computers came along. The mini-computer didn't solve all the problems of a mainframe, but it turned out that for many applications those problems weren't all that important. Programming languages, too, go through waves where they get more complex and then simpler. C begets C++, which begets Java, which is now becoming itself more complicated.

Pursuing simplicity enables innovation. JUnit was much simpler than the testing tools it largely replaced. JUnit spawned a variety of look-alikes, add-ons, and new programming/testing techniques. The latest release, JUnit 4, has lost that "bare metal" feel, although I made or concurred with each of the complexifying decisions. Someday someone will come up with a much simpler way for programmers to write tests than JUnit. The new idea will enable a further wave of innovation.

Apply simplicity at all levels. Format code so no code can be deleted without losing information. Design with no extraneous elements. Challenge requirements to find those that are essential. Eliminating excess complexity illuminates the remaining code, giving you a chance to approach it afresh.

Communication and simplicity often work together. The less excess complexity, the easier a system is to understand. The more you focus on communication, the easier it is to see what complexity can be discarded. Sometimes, however, I find a simplification that would make a program harder to understand. I choose communication over simplicity in these cases. Such situations are rare but usually point to some larger-scale simplification I'm not yet seeing.

Flexibility

Of the three values listed here, flexibility is the justification used for the most ineffective coding and design practices. To retrieve a constant, I've seen programs look up an environment variable containing the name of a directory containing a file in which is found the constant value. Why all the complexity? Flexibility. Programs should be flexible, but only in ways they change. If the constant never changes, all that complexity is cost without benefit.

Since most of the cost of a program will be incurred after it is first deployed, programs should be easy to change. The flexibility I imagine will be needed tomorrow, though, is likely to be not what I need when I change the code. That's why the flexibility of simplicity and extensive tests is more effective than the flexibility offered by speculative design.

Choose patterns that encourage flexibility and bring immediate benefits. For patterns with immediate costs and only deferred benefits, often patience is the best strategy. Put them back in the bag until they are needed. Then you can apply them in precisely the way they are needed.

Flexibility can come at the cost of increased complexity. For instance, user-configurable options provide flexibility but add the complexity of a configuration file and the need to take the options into account when programming. Simplicity can encourage flexibility. In the above example, if you can find a way to eliminate the configurable options without losing value, you will have a program that is easier to change later.

Enhancing the communicability of software also adds to flexibility. The more people who can quickly read, understand, and modify the code, the more options your organization has for future change.

The patterns that follow encourage flexibility by helping programmers create simple, understandable applications that can be changed.

Principles

The implementation patterns aren't the way they are "just because". Each one expresses one or more of the values of communication, simplicity, and flexibility. Principles are another level of general ideas, more specific to programming than the values, that also form the foundation of the patterns.

Examining principles is valuable for several reasons. Clear principles can lead to new patterns, just as the periodic table of the elements led to the discovery of new elements. Principles can provide an explanation for the motivation behind a pattern, one connected to general rather than specific ideas. Choices about contradictory patterns are often best discussed in terms of principles rather than the specifics of the patterns involved. Finally, understanding principles provides a guide when encountering novel situations.

For example, when I encounter a new programming language I use my understanding of principles to develop an effective style of programming. I don't have to ape existing styles or, worse, cling to my style in some other programming language (you can write FORTRAN code in any language, but you shouldn't). Understanding principles gives me a chance to learn quickly and act with integrity in novel situations. What follows is the list of principles behind the implementation patterns.

Local Consequences

Structure the code so changes have local consequences. If a change *here* can cause a problem *there*, then the cost of the change rises dramatically. Code with mostly local consequences communicates effectively. It can be understood gradually without first having to assemble an understanding of the whole.

Because keeping the cost of making changes low is a primary motivation behind the implementation patterns, the principle of local consequences is part of the reasoning behind many of the patterns.

Minimize Repetition

A principle that contributes to keeping consequences local is to minimize repetition. When you have the same code in several places, if you change one copy of the code you have to decide whether or not to change all the other copies. Your change is no longer local. The more copies of the code, the more a change will cost.

Copied code is only one form of repetition. Parallel class hierarchies are also repetitive, and break the principle of local consequences. If making one conceptual change requires me to change two or more class hierarchies, then the changes have spreading consequences. Restructuring so the changes are again local would improve the code.

Duplication is not always obvious until after it has been created, and sometimes not for a while even then. Having seen it I can't always think of a good way to eliminate it. Duplication isn't evil, it just raises the cost of making changes.

One of the ways to remove duplication is to break programs up into many small pieces—small statements, small methods, small objects, small packages. Large pieces of logic tend to duplicate parts of other large pieces of logic. This commonality is what makes patterns possible—while there are differences between different pieces of code, there are also many similarities. Clearly communicating which parts of programs are identical, which parts are merely similar, and which parts are completely different makes programs easier to read and cheaper to modify.

Logic and Data Together

Another principle corollary to the principle of local consequences is keeping logic and data together. Put logic and the data it operates on near each other, in the same method if possible, or the same object, or at least the same package. To make a change, the logic and data are likely to have to change at the same time. If they are together, then the consequences of changing them will remain local.

It's not always obvious at first where logic or data should go to satisfy this principle. I may be writing code in A and realize I need data from B. It's only after I have the code working that I notice that it is too far from the data. Then

I need to choose what to do: move the code to the data, move the data to the code, put the code and data together in a helper object, or realize I can't at the moment think of how to bring them together in a way that communicates effectively.

Symmetry

Another principle I use all the time is symmetry. Symmetries abound in programs. An add() method is accompanied by a remove() method. A group of methods all take the same parameters. All the fields in an object have the same lifetime. Identifying and clearly expressing symmetry makes code easier to read. Once readers understand one half of the symmetry, they can quickly understand the other half.

Symmetry is often discussed in spatial terms: bilateral, rotational, and so on. Symmetry in programs is seldom graphical, it is conceptual. Symmetry in code is where the same idea is expressed the same way everywhere it appears in the code.

Here's an example of code that lacks symmetry:

```
void process() {
  input();
  count++;
  output();
}
```

The second statement is more concrete than the two messages. I would rewrite this on the basis of symmetry, resulting in:

```
void process() {
  input();
  incrementCount();
  output();
}
```

Still this method violates symmetry. The input() and output() operations are named after intentions, incrementCount() after an implementation. Looking for symmetries, I think about *why* I am incrementing the count, perhaps resulting in:

```
void process() {
  input();
  tally();
  output();
}
```

Often, finding and expressing symmetry is a preliminary step to removing duplication. If a similar thought exists in several places in the code, making them symmetrical to each other is a good first step towards unifying them.

Declarative Expression

Another principle behind the implementation patterns is to express as much of my intention as possible declaratively. Imperative programming is powerful and flexible, but to read it requires that you follow the thread of execution. I must build a model in my head of the state of the program and the flow of control and data. For those parts of a program that are more like simple facts, without sequence or conditionals, it is easier to read code that is simply declarative.

For example, in older versions of JUnit, classes could have a static suite() method that returned a set of tests to run.

```
public static junit.framework.Test suite() {
  Test result= new TestSuite();
  ...complicated stuff...
  return result;
}
```

Now comes the simple, common question—what tests are going to be run? In most cases, the suite() method just aggregates the tests in a bunch of classes. However, because the suite() method is general, I have to go read and understand the method if I want to be sure.

JUnit 4, on the other hand, uses the principle of declarative expression to solve the same problem. Instead of a method returning a suite of tests, there is a special test runner that runs the tests in a set of classes (the common case):

```
@RunWith(Suite.class)
@TestClasses({
  SimpleTest.class,
  ComplicatedTest.class
})
class AllTests {
}
```

If I know that tests are being aggregated using this method, I only need to look at the TestClasses annotation to see what tests will be run. Because the expression of the suite is declarative I don't need to suspect any tricky exceptions. This solution gives up the power and generality of the original suite() method, but the declarative style makes the code easier to read. (The RunWith annotation provides even more flexibility for running tests than the suite() method, but that's a story for a different book.)

Rate of Change

A final principle is to put logic or data that changes at the same rate together and separate logic or data that changes at different rates. These rates of change are a form of temporal symmetry. Sometimes the rate of change principle applies to changes a programmer makes. For example, if I am writing tax software I will separate code that makes general tax calculations from code that is particular to a given year. The code changes at different rates. When I make changes the following year, I would like to be sure that the code from preceding years still works. Separating them gives me more confidence in the local consequences of my changes.

The rate of change applies to data. All the fields in a single object should change at roughly the same rate. For example, fields that are modified only during the activation of a single method should be local variables. Two fields that change together but out of sync with their neighboring fields probably belong in a helper object. If a financial instrument can have its value and currency change together, then those two fields would probably better be expressed as a helper Money object:

```
setAmount(int value, String currency) {
  this.value= value;
  this.currency= currency;
}
```

becomes:

```
setAmount(int value, String currency) {
  this.value= new Money(value, currency);
}
```

and then later:

```
setAmount(Money value) {
  this.value= value;
}
```

The rate of change principle is an application of symmetry, but temporal symmetry. In the example above, the two original fields value and currency are symmetrical. They change at the same time. However, they are not symmetrical with the other fields in the object. Expressing the symmetry by putting them in their own object communicates their relationship to readers and is likely to set up further opportunities to reduce duplication and further localize consequences later.

Conclusion

This chapter has introduced the theoretical foundations of the implementation patterns. The values of communication, simplicity, and flexibility provide wide-ranging motivation for the patterns. The principles of local consequences, minimize repetition, logic and data together, symmetry, declarative expression, and rate of change help translate the values into action. Now we come to the patterns, specific solutions to repeating tactical problems in programming.

The next chapter, "Motivation", describes the economic factors that make focusing on communication through code a valuable activity.

Chapter 4

Motivation

Thirty years ago Yourdon and Constantine in *Structured Design* identified economics as the underlying driver of software design. Software should be designed to reduce its overall cost. The cost of software is divided into the initial cost and the cost of maintenance:

$$cost_{total} = cost_{develop} + cost_{maintain}$$

Once the industry gained experience with software development, it was a big surprise to many that the cost of maintenance is much higher than the cost of initial development. (Projects with little or no maintenance should use a very different set of implementation patterns from those presented in the remainder of this book.)

Maintenance is expensive because understanding existing code is time-consuming and error-prone. Making changes is generally easy when you know what needs changing. Learning what the current code does is the expensive part. Once the changes are made, they need to be tested and deployed.

$$cost_{maintain} = cost_{understand} + cost_{change} + cost_{test} + cost_{deploy}$$

One strategy for reducing overall cost is to invest more in initial development in hope of reducing or eliminating the need for maintenance. Such efforts have generally failed to reduce overall costs. When code needs to change in unanticipated ways, no amount of forethought can perfectly prepare the code for change. The premature attempts to make the code general enough to meet future needs often interfere with the unanticipated changes that turn out to be necessary.

Substantially increasing the up-front investment in software runs counter to two important economic principles: the time value of money and the uncertainty of the future. Since a dollar today is worth more than a dollar tomorrow, in principle an implementation strategy should generally encourage deferring costs. Also, because of uncertainty an implementation strategy should generally take immediate benefits in preference over possible long-term benefits. While this may sound like a license to hack without regard for the future, the implementation patterns are focused on ways to gain immediate benefit while setting up clean code for ease of future development.

My strategy for reducing overall costs is to ask all programmers to address the cost of understanding code during the maintenance phase by focusing on communicating, programmer-to-programmer. The immediate benefits of clear code are fewer defects, easier sharing of code, and smoother development.

Once a set of implementation patterns has become habitual, I program faster and with fewer distracting thoughts. When I began writing my first set of implementation patterns (*The Smalltalk Best Practice Patterns*, Prentice Hall 1996) I thought I was a proficient programmer. To encourage myself to focus on patterns, I refused to type a character of code unless I had first written down the pattern I was following. It was frustrating, like I was coding with my fingers glued together. For the first week every minute of coding was preceded by an hour of writing. The second week I found I had most of the basic patterns in place and most of the time I was following existing patterns. By the third week I was coding much faster than I had before, because I had carefully looked at my own style and I wasn't nagged by doubts.

The implementation patterns that I wrote down were only partly my own invention. Most of my style was copied from earlier generations of programmers. They were the habits that resulted in code that was easier to read, understand, and modify, and by codifying them I was able to code more quickly and fluidly than I had before. I could prepare for the future and get today's code done faster at the same time.

For the implementation patterns in this book I looked at existing code as well as my own habits for inspiration. I read and compared code from the JDK, from Eclipse, and from my experience of development. The resulting patterns are intended to be a coherent view of how to write code people can understand. Other points of view or sets of values would result in different patterns. For example, I sketch the implementation patterns for framework development in "Evolving Frameworks". These are based on a different set of priorities and so vary from my basic implementation style.

The implementation patterns serve human as well as economic needs. Code is by people and for people. Programmers can use the implementation patterns to help satisfy human needs, like the need to take pride in work well done or the need to be a trustworthy member of a community. I discuss the human and economic impact of the patterns as we go in the following chapters.

Chapter 5

Class

The idea of classes goes back long before Plato. The platonic solids were classes, instances of which could be seen in the world. The platonic sphere was absolutely perfect but insubstantial. The spheres around us we could touch, but they were all imperfect in some way.

Object-oriented programming picked up on this idea by way of later western philosophers, dividing programs into classes, which are general descriptions of a whole set of similar things, and objects, which are the things themselves.

Classes are important for communication because they describe, potentially, many specific things. Class-level patterns have the largest span of any of the implementation patterns. Design patterns, by contrast, generally talk about the relationships between classes.

The following patterns appear in this chapter:

- Class—Use a class to say, "This data goes together and this logic goes with it."

- Simple Superclass Name—Name the roots of class hierarchies with simple names drawn from the same metaphor.

- Qualified Subclass Name—Name subclasses to communicate the similarities and differences with a superclass.

- Abstract Interface—Separate the interface from the implementation.

- Interface—Specify an abstract interface which doesn't change often with a Java interface.

- Versioned Interface—Extend interfaces safely by introducing a new sub-interface.

- Abstract Class—Specify an abstract interface which will likely change with an abstract class.

21

- Value Object—Write an object that acts like a mathematical value.

- Specialization—Clearly express the similarities and differences of related computations.

- Subclass—Express one-dimensional variation with a subclass.

- Implementor—Override a method to express a variant of a computation.

- Inner Class—Bundle locally useful code in a private class.

- Instance-specific Behavior—Vary logic by instance.

- Conditional—Vary logic by explicit conditionals.

- Delegation—Vary logic by delegating to one of several types of objects.

- Pluggable Selector—Vary logic by reflectively executing a method.

- Anonymous Inner Class—Vary logic by overriding one or two methods right in the method that is creating a new object.

- Library Class—Represent a bundle of functionality that doesn't fit into any object as a set of static methods.

Class

Data changes more frequently than logic. That is the observation that makes classes work. Each class is a declaration, "This logic goes together and changes more slowly than the data values on which it operates. These data values also go together, changing at similar rates and being operated on by related logic." This strict separation between data-that-changes and logic-that-does-not-change isn't absolute. Sometimes the logic will be a little different based on data values; sometimes the logic varies considerably. Sometimes data doesn't change in the course of a computation. Learning how to bundle logic in classes and express variations in that logic is part of programming effectively with objects.

Organizing classes into hierarchies is a form of compression, taking the superclass and including it textually in all the subclasses. As with all compression techniques, it leaves the code more difficult to read. You have to understand the context of the superclass to be able to understand the subclass.

Using inheritance judiciously is another aspect of programming effectively with objects. Creating a subclass says, "I'm like that superclass, only different." (Isn't it strange that we speak of *overriding* a method in a *subclass*? How much better programmers would we be if we had thoughtfully selected our metaphors?)

Classes are relatively expensive design elements in programs built from objects. A class should do something significant. Reducing the number of classes in a system is an improvement, as long as the remaining classes do not become bloated.

The patterns that follow explain how to communicate by declaring classes.

Simple Superclass Name

Finding just the right name is one of the most satisfying moments in programming. You're struggling with an idea. Oftentimes, the code has gotten complicated and it doesn't seem like it needs to be. Then, often in conversation, someone says, "Oh, I see! This is really a Scheduler." Everyone sits back and lets out a breath. The right name results in a cascade of further simplifications and improvements.

Some of the most important names to choose well are those of classes. Classes are the central anchoring concept in the design. Once classes have been named, the names of operations follow. It is rare for the reverse to be true, except if the class was poorly named in the first place.

In naming classes there is a tension between brevity and expressiveness. You'll be using class names in conversation: "Did you remember to rotate the Figure before translating it?" The names should be short and punchy. However, to make the names precise sometimes seems to require several words.

A way out of this dilemma is picking a strong metaphor for the computation. With a metaphor in mind, even single words bring with them a rich web of associations, connections, and implications. For example, in the HotDraw drawing framework, my first name for an object in a drawing was DrawingObject. Ward Cunningham came along with the typography metaphor: a drawing is like a printed, laid-out page. Graphical items on a page are figures, so the class became Figure. In the context of the metaphor, Figure is simultaneously shorter, richer, and more precise than DrawingObject.

Sometimes, good names take time to find. You may have code "done" and working for weeks, months, or (in one notable case for me) years when you discover a better name for a class. Sometimes you need to push a little harder to find a name: pull out a thesaurus, write down a list of the least-suitable names you can think of, take a walk. Sometimes you need to forge ahead with new functionality, trusting time, frustration, and your subconscious to supply a better name.

Conversation is a tool that consistently helps me find better names. Explaining the purpose of an object to another person leads me to look for rich and evocative images to describe it. These images can lead in turn to new names.

Look for one-word names for important classes.

Qualified Subclass Name

The names of subclasses have two jobs. They need to communicate what class they are *like* and how they are *different*. Again, the balance to be struck is between length and expressiveness. Unlike the names at the roots of hierarchies, subclass names aren't used nearly as often in conversation, so they can be expressive at the cost of being concise. Prepend one or more modifiers to the superclass name to form a subclass name.

One exception to this rule is when subclassing is used strictly as an implementation sharing mechanism and the subclass is an important concept in its own right. Give subclasses that serve as the roots of hierarchies their own simple names. For example, HotDraw has a class Handle which presents figure-editing operations when a figure is selected. It is called, simply, Handle in spite of extending Figure. There is a whole family of handles and they most appropriately have names like StretchyHandle and TransparencyHandle. Because Handle is the root of its own hierarchy, it deserves a simple superclass name more than a qualified subclass name.

Another wrinkle in subclass naming is multiple-level hierarchies. Multi-level hierarchies are usually delegation waiting to happen, but while they exist they need good names. Rather than blindly prepend the modifiers to the immediate superclass, think about the name from the reader's perspective. What class does he need to know this class is like? Use that superclass as the basis for the subclass name.

Communication with people is the purpose of class names. As far as the computer is concerned, classes could simply be numbered. Class names that are too long are hard to read and format. Class names that are too short tax the reader's short-term memory. Clusters of classes whose names don't relate to each other will be difficult to comprehend and recall. Use class names to tell the story of your code.

Abstract Interface

The old adage in software development is to code to interfaces, not implementations. This is another way of suggesting that a design decision should not be visible in more places than necessary. If most of my code only knows that I am dealing with a collection I am free to change the concrete class later. However, at some point you actually have to commit to a concrete class so the computer can perform a calculation.

By "interface" here I mean "a set of operations without implementations". This can be represented in Java either as an interface or as a superclass. Patterns below will suggest when each is appropriate.

Every layer of interface has costs. It is one more thing to learn, understand, document, debug, organize, browse, and name. Maximizing the number of interfaces doesn't minimize the cost of software. Pay for interfaces only where you will need the flexibility they create. Since you can't often know in advance where you will need the flexibility of an interface, to minimize cost, combine speculating about where to introduce interfaces with adding them when flexibility is required.

Much as we complain about the inflexibility of software, there are a very large number of ways we don't need any given system to flex. From fundamental changes like the number of bits in an integer to large-scale changes like new business models, most software doesn't need to be flexible in most of the ways it could be.

Another economic factor in introducing interfaces is the unpredictability of software. Our industry seems addicted to the idea that if only we designed software right we would not have to change our systems. I recently read a list of reasons software changes. On the list were programmers doing a bad job of eliciting requirements, sponsors changing their mind, and on and on. The one factor that was missing from the list was legitimate change. The list assumed change was always a mistake. Why won't one weather forecast do for all time? Because the weather changes in unpredictable ways. Why can't we list once and for all the ways a system needs to be flexible? Because the requirements change in unpredictable ways and technology changes in unpredictable ways. This doesn't relieve us from the responsibility to do our best to develop the system customers need right now, but it suggests that there are limits to the value of "future-proofing" software through speculation.

Putting all of these factors together—the need for flexibility, the cost of flexibility, the unpredictability of where flexibility is needed—leads me to the belief that the time to introduce flexibility is when it is definitely needed. Introducing flexibility costs because of the changes you need to make to existing software. If you can't personally change all the software that needs to change, the costs rise further, a topic taken up in detail in the chapter on evolving frameworks.

Java's two mechanisms for abstract interfaces, superclasses and interfaces, have different cost profiles for such changes.

Interface

One way of saying "Here's what I want to accomplish and beyond that are details that shouldn't concern me" is to declare a Java interface. Interfaces are one of the important innovations first put in a mass-market language in Java. Interfaces are a nice balance. They have some of the flexibility of multiple inheritance without the complexity and ambiguity. One class can declare itself as participating in multiple interfaces. Interfaces reveal only operations, not fields, so they can effectively protect users of an interface from changes in implementation.

If interfaces enable changes to their implementations, they discourage changes to the interface itself. Any addition or change to an interface requires modifying all implementors. If you can't modify the implementations, widespread use of interfaces provides significant drag on further design evolution.

One quirk of interfaces that limits their value as a way to communicate is that all operations are required to be public. I have often wished for package-visible operations in interfaces. Making design elements a little too public isn't a problem when they are for private use, but when publishing interfaces to a large audience it would be better to be able to be precise rather than build up inertia against future change.

Two styles of naming interfaces depend on how you are thinking of the interfaces. Interfaces as classes without implementations should be named as if they were classes (Simple Superclass Name, Qualified Subclass Name). One problem with this style of naming is that the good names are used up before you get to naming classes. An interface called File needs an implementation class called something like ActualFile, ConcreteFile, or (yuck!) FileImpl (both a suffix and an abbreviation). In general, communicating whether one is dealing with a concrete or abstract object is important, whether the abstract object is implemented as an interface or a superclass is less important. Deferring the distinction between interfaces and superclasses is well supported by this style of naming, leaving you free to change your mind later if that becomes necessary.

Sometimes, naming concrete classes simply is more important to communication than hiding the use of interfaces. In this case, prefix interface names with "I". If the interface is called IFile, the class can be simply called File.

Abstract Class

The other way to express the distinction between abstract interface and concrete implementation in Java is to use a superclass. The superclass is abstract in the sense that it can be replaced at runtime with any subclass, whether it is abstract in the Java sense or not.

The trade-offs for when to use an abstract class versus an interface boil down to two issues: changes to the interface and the need for a single class to support multiple interfaces simultaneously. Abstract interfaces need to support two kinds of change: change in the implementation and change of the interface itself. Java interfaces do a poor job of supporting the latter. Every change to an interface requires changes to all implementations. With a widely implemented interface, this can easily lead to paralysis of existing designs, with further evolution only available through versioned interfaces.

Abstract classes do not suffer this limitation. As long as a default implementation can be specified, new operations can be added to an abstract class without disrupting existing implementors.

One limitation of abstract classes is that implementors can only declare their allegiance to one superclass. If other views of the same class are necessary, they must be implementated by Java interfaces.

Using the keyword abstract with a class tells readers that they will have to do some implementation work if they want to use the class. If there is any chance to make the root of a class hierarchy useful and instantiable on its own, do so. Once on the path of abstraction, it is easy to go too far and create abstractions that never pay off. Striving to make root classes instantiable encourages you to eliminate abstractions that are unlikely to pull their weight.

Interfaces and class hierarchies are not mutually exclusive. You can provide an interface which says, "Here's how to access this kind of functionality," and a superclass which says, "Here's one way to implement this functionality." In this case, variables should be declared with the interface as their type so future maintainers are free to substitute new implementations as necessary.

Versioned Interface

What do you do when you need to change an interface but you can't? Typically this happens when you want to add operations. Since adding an operation will break all existing implementors, you can't do that. However, you can declare a new interface that extends the original interface and add the operation there. Users who want the new functionality use the extended interface while existing users remain oblivious to the existence of the new interface. Anywhere you want to access the new operation you must explicitly check the type of your object and downcast to the new type.

For example, consider a simple command:

```
interface Command {
  void run();
}
```

Once this interface has been published and extended a thousand times, changing it becomes expensive. However, to support undoing of commands you need a new operation. The versioned interface style of solution is this:

```
interface ReversibleCommand extends Command {
  void undo();
}
```

Existing instances of Command work as before. Instances of ReversibleCommand work anywhere a Command works. To use the new operation, downcast:

```
...
Command recent= ...;
if (recent instanceof ReversibleCommand) {
  ReversibleCommand downcasted= (ReversibleCommand) recent;
  downcasted.undo();
]
...
```

Using instanceof generally reduces flexibility by tying code to certain classes. In this case, however, it may be justified because it enables the evolution of interfaces. If you begin to have several alternative interfaces, however, clients need to do a lot of work to deal with all the variations. These are signs that it is time to rethink the design.

Alternative interfaces are an ugly solution to an ugly problem. Interfaces don't accommodate change to their structure as easily as they accommodate change to their implementations. Interfaces are likely to change, just like all design decisions. We all learn about design through implementation and maintenance. Alternative interfaces create a new programming language that is like Java but with new rules. Writing new languages is a different game with tougher rules than writing applications. However, if you are stuck in the situation of needing to extend an interface, it's nice to know how.

Value Object

While objects-with-changing-state is one valuable way to think about computation, it is not the only way to think. Mathematics has developed over millennia as a way to think about situations that can be reduced to an abstract world of absolute truth and certainty, where statements can be made about eternal verities.

Our current programming languages are a mix of the two styles. The so-called primitive types in Java belong (mostly) to the world of mathematics.

When I add 1 to a number in Java, I am making a statement of mathematics (all except that part where someone decided my computer only had to count up to 2^{32} or 2^{64} and then we should let it start over). I don't change the value of a variable when I add 1: I create a new value. There is no way to change 0, as you can with most objects.

This functional style of computing never changes any state, it only creates new values. When you have a (perhaps momentarily) static situation about which you'd like to make statements or about which you'd like to ask questions, then the functional style is appropriate. When the situation is changing over time, then state is appropriate. Some situations could be thought of in either way. How can you tell which way is most helpful?

For example, you can represent drawing a picture as changes to the state of some graphics medium like a bitmap. Alternatively, you can describe the same picture with a static description (Figure 5.1).

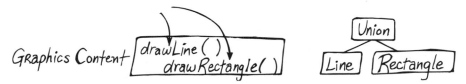

Figure 5.1 *Graphics represented as procedures and objects*

Which of these representations is most useful depends to some extent on personal preference, but it also depends on the complexity of the pictures to be drawn and how often they change.

Procedural interfaces are more common than functional interfaces. One problem with procedural interfaces is that the sequence of procedure calls becomes an important (but often implicit) part of the meaning of the interface. Changing such a program is touchy and difficult because seemingly small changes have unintended consequences when the implicit meaning of the sequence is changed.

The beauty of mathematical representations is that sequence seldom matters. You are creating a world in which you can make absolute, timeless statements. Create micro-worlds of mathematics wherever possible. Manage them from an object with changing state.

For example, implement an accounting system by making the basic transactions unchanging mathematical values.

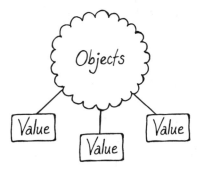

Figure 5.2   *State-changing objects referring to immutable objects at the edges*

```
class Transaction {
  int value;
  Transaction(int value, Account credit, Account debit) {
    this.value= value;
    credit.addCredit(this);
    debit.addDebit(this);
  }
  int getValue() {
    return value;
  }
}
```

There is no way to change any of the values of a Transaction once it has been created. What's more, the constructor makes the statement that all transactions are posted to two accounts. When I read this code, I know that I don't have to worry about transactions floating around loose or about transactions having their values changed after they have been posted.

To implement value-style objects (that is, objects that act like integers rather than like holders of changing state), first draw the boundary between the world of state and the world of value. In the example above, a Transaction is a value, an Account holds changing state. Set all state in a value-style object in the constructor, with no other field assignments elsewhere in the object. Operations on value-style objects always return new objects. These objects must be stored by the requestor of the operation.

```
bounds.translateBy(10, 20); // mutable Rectangle
bounds= bounds.translateBy(10, 20); // value-style Rectangle
```

The biggest argument against value-style objects has always been performance. The need to create all those intermediate objects can put a strain on the memory management system. In the overall cost of programming, this argument doesn't often hold up because most parts of the program are not performance bottlenecks. Other reasons not to use value-style objects are unfamiliarity with the style and difficulty drawing boundaries between parts of the system where state changes and parts of the system where objects don't change. Objects that are mostly value-style are the worst of both worlds, since the interfaces tend to be more complicated but you can't safely make assumptions about state not changing.

Having gotten this far, I sense that there is much more to be written about programming with the three main styles—objects, functions, and procedures—and how to blend them effectively. For purposes of this book, I'll close by reiterating that sometimes your programs will best be expressed as a combination of state-changing objects and objects representing mathematical values.

Specialization

Communicating the interplay between the similarities and differences of computations makes your programs easier to read, use, and modify. In practice, each program is not unique. Many express similar ideas, and, often, many parts of the same program express similar ideas. Expressing similarities and differences clearly allows readers to understand the existing code, discover if their current intentions are covered by one of the existing variations, or, if not, how to best either specialize the existing code to their needs or write entirely new code.

The simplest variations are those where state differs. The string "abc" is different from "def". The algorithms that operate on the two strings are identical. For example, the length of all strings is calculated in the same way.

The most complex variations are total differences in logic. A symbolic integration routine has no logic in common with a mathematical typesetting routine, even though the two might share exactly the same input.

In between these two extremes—identical logic with different data and different logic with identical data—lies the huge common ground of programming. Data can be mostly the same but a little different. Logic can be mostly the same but a little different. (I would guess that the symbolic integration routine and the mathematical typesetting routine share little code.) Even the line between logic and data is blurry. A flag is boolean data but it affects the flow of control. A helper object can be stored in a field but used to affect a computation.

The patterns that follow are a variety of techniques to communicate similarity and difference, primarily in logic. Variations in data don't seem as complicated or subtle. Effective expressions of similarity and difference in logic open up new opportunities for further expansion of the code.

Subclass

Declaring a subclass is a way of saying, "These objects are like those except..." If you have the right superclass, creating a subclass can be a powerful way to program. With the right method to override, you can introduce a variant of an existing calculation with a few lines of code.

When objects first became popular, subclassing seemed like a magic pill. First, subclasses were used for classification—a Train was a subclass of Vehicle regardless of whether they shared any implementation. In time, some people saw that since what inheritance did was share implementation, it could most effectively be used to factor out common bits of implementation. Quickly, though, the limitations of subclassing became apparent. First, it's a card you can only play once. If you discover that some set of variations isn't well expressed as subclasses, you have some work to do to disentangle the code before you can restructure it. Second, you have to understand the superclass before you can understand the subclass. As the superclasses become more complicated this becomes more of a limitation. Third, changes to a superclass are risky, since subclasses can rely on subtle properties of the superclass's implementation. Finally, all of these problems are compounded by deep inheritance hierarchies.

A particularly pernicious use of inheritance is creating parallel hierarchies, where for each subclass in *this* hierarchy you need a subclass in *that* hierarchy. This is a form of duplication, creating implicit coupling between the class hierarchies. To successfully introduce a new variation you need to change both hierarchies. While I often see parallel hierarchies that I can't immediately figure out how to eliminate, the effort to do so improves the design.

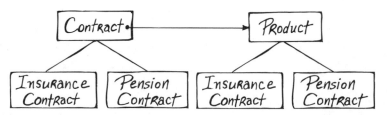

Figure 5.3   *Parallel hierarchies*

One example of this was an insurance system (Figure 5.3). Something is definitely wrong with this picture, because an InsuranceContract cannot refer to a PensionProduct nor is it attractive to move the product field down to the subclasses. The solution, which we never reached but took a year to come close to, was to move the variation around so Contract worked the same whether it was used for insurance or a pension. This required creating a new object to represent the prospective cash flows (Figure 5.4).

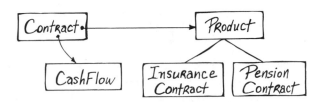

Figure 5.4 *Hierarchy with duplication eliminated*

With all these warnings in mind, subclassing can be a powerful tool for expressing theme-and-variations computations. The right subclass can help many people to express exactly the computation they want with a method or two. One key to achieving useful subclasses is to thoroughly factor the logic in the superclass into methods that do one job. When writing a subclass, you should be able to override exactly one method. If the superclass methods are too big, you'll have to copy code and edit it (Figure 5.5).

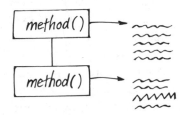

Figure 5.5 *Code copied and modified in a subclass*

Copied code introduces an ugly implicit coupling between the two classes. You can't safely change the code in the superclass without examining and potentially changing all the places to which it has been copied.

My goal in design is to be able to switch between strategies at will, depending on the needs of the code as it now exists. Visualize the code expressed with conditionals, with subclasses, with delegation. Does it seem like there are advantages to a different strategy than the one you are currently using? Take a few steps in that direction and see if you improve the code.

A final limitation of subclassing is that it cannot be used to express changing logic. The variation you want must be known when you create an object and can't be changed thereafter. You'll need to use conditionals or delegation to express logic that changes.

Implementor

The polymorphic message is the fundamental way to express a choice in a program built from objects. For the message to do its work of choosing, there needs to be more than one kind of object to potentially receive the message.

Implementing the same protocol multiple times, whether expressed with a Java interface and an implements declaration or as a subclass expressed with extends, is a way of saying, "From the point of view of one part of the calculation, as long as something happens matching the intention of the code, the details of what happens are irrelevant."

The beauty of polymorphic messages is that they open a system to variation. If a part of the program writes some bytes to another system, the introduction of an abstract Socket enables the implementation of the socket to vary without affecting the calling code. Compared to the procedural expression of the same intention, with its explicit and closed conditional logic, the object/message version is clearer, separating the expression of the intention (write some bytes) from the implementation (call a TCP/IP stack with certain parameters). At the same time, expressing the computation as objects and messages opens the system to future variation undreamt of by the original programmers. This fortuitous combination of clarity of expression and flexibility is why object languages have become the dominant programming paradigm.

This supreme resource is easy to squander by writing procedural programs in Java. The patterns here are intended to help you express logic that is both clear and extendable.

Inner Class

Sometimes you need to package part of a computation but you don't want to incur the cost of a whole new class with its own file. Declaring small, private classes (inner classes) gives you a low-cost way of having many of the benefits of a class without all of its costs.

Sometimes an inner class extends only Object. Some inner classes extend another superclass, which is useful for expressing refinements of other classes that are only locally interesting.

One of the features of inner classes is that when their instances are created, they are secretly passed a copy of the object that is creating them. This is handy when you want to access the enclosing instance's data without making the relationship between the two classes explicit:

```java
public class InnerClassExample {
  private String field;

  public class Inner {
    public String example() {
      return field; // Uses the field from the enclosing instance
    }

  @Test public void passes() {
    field= "abc";
    Inner bar= new Inner();
    assertEquals("abc", bar.example());
  }
}
```

However, in the inner class above, there is not really a no-arg constructor, even if you declare one. This is a problem when creating instances of inner classes by reflection.

```java
public class InnerClassExample {
  public class Inner {
    public Inner() {
    }
  }

  @Test(expected=NoSuchMethodException.class)
  public void innerHasNoNoArgConstructor() throws Exception {
    Inner.class.getConstructor(new Class[0]);
  }
}
```

To get an inner class that is completely detached from its enclosing instances, declare it static.

Instance-Specific Behavior

In theory, all instances of a class share the same logic. Relaxing this constraint enables new styles of expression. All of these styles, though, come at a cost. When the logic of an object is completely determined by its class, readers can read the code in the class to see what is going to happen. Once you have instances with different behavior, you have to look at live examples or analyze the data flow to understand how a particular object is going to behave.

Another step up in the cost of instance-specific behavior is when the logic changes as the computation progresses. For ease of code reading, try to set instance-specific behavior when an object is created and don't change it afterward.

Conditional

If/then and switch statements are the simplest form of instance-specific behavior. Using conditionals, different objects will execute different logic based on their data. Conditionals as a form of expression have the advantage that the logic is still all in one class. Readers don't have to go navigating around to find the possible paths for a computation. However, conditionals have the disadvantage that they can't be modified except by modifying the code of the object in question.

Each path of execution through a program has some probability of being correct. Assuming that the probabilities of correctness for the paths are independent, the more paths through a program the less likely the program is to be correct. The probabilities aren't entirely independent, but they are independent enough that programs with many paths are more likely to have defects than those with few paths. The proliferation of conditionals reduces reliability.

This problem is compounded when conditionals are duplicated. Consider a simple graphic editor. The figures will need a display() method:

```
public void display() {
  switch (getType()) {
    case RECTANGLE :
      //...
      break;
    case OVAL :
      //...
      break;
    case TEXT :
      //...
      break;
    default :
```

```
      break;
   }
}
```

Figures will also need a method to determine whether a point is contained within them:

```
public boolean contains(Point p) {
  switch (getType()) {
    case RECTANGLE :
      //...
      break;
    case OVAL :
      //...
      break;
    case TEXT :
      //...
      break;
    default :
      break;
  }
}
```

Suppose now you want to add a new kind of figure. First, you must add a clause to every switch statement. Second, to make this change you have to modify the Figure class, putting all of the existing functionality at risk. Lastly, everyone who wants to add new figures must coordinate their changes of a single class.

These problems can all be eliminated by converting the conditional logic to messages, either with subclasses or delegation (which technique serves best depends on the code). Duplicate conditional logic or logic where the processing is very different based on which branch of a conditional is taken is generally better expressed as messages instead of explicit logic. Also, conditional logic that changes frequently is better expressed as messages to simplify changing one branch while minimizing the effects on other branches.

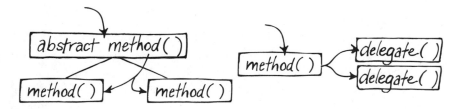

Figure 5.6 *Conditional logic represented by subclasses and delegation*

In short, the strengths of conditionals—that they are simple and local—
become liabilities when they are used too widely.

Delegation

Another way to execute different logic in different instances is to delegate work
to one of several possible kinds of objects. The common logic is held in the
referring class, the variations in the delegates.

An example of using a delegate to capture variation is handling user input in
a graphical editor. Sometimes a button press means "create a rectangle",
sometimes it means "move a figure", and so on.

One way to express the variation between the tools is with conditional logic:

```
public void mouseDown() {
  switch (getTool()) {
    case SELECTING :
      //...
      break;
    case CREATING_RECTANGLE :
      //...
      break;
    case EDITING_TEXT :
      //...
      break;
    default :
      break;
  }
}
```

This has all the problems of conditionals discussed above: adding a new tool
requires modifying the code and the duplication of the conditional (in mouseUp(),
mouseMove(), etc.) makes adding new tools complicated.

Subclassing is not an immediate answer either because the editor needs to
change tools during its lifetime. Delegation allows that flexibility.

```
public void mouseDown() {
  getTool().mouseDown();
}
```

The code that used to live in the clauses of the switch statement is moved to
the various tools. Now new tools can be introduced without modifying the
code of the editor or the existing tools. Reading the code requires more
navigation, however, because the mouse-down logic is spread over several
classes. Understanding how the editor will behave in a given situation requires
that you understand what kind of tool it is currently using.

Delegates can be stored in fields (a "pluggable object"), but they can also be computed on the fly. JUnit 4 dynamically computes the object that will run the tests in a given class. If a class contains old-style tests, one delegate is created, but if the class contains new-style tests, a different delegate is created. This is a mix of conditional logic (to create the delegates) and delegation.

Delegation can be used for code sharing as well as instance-specific behavior. An object that delegates to a Stream may be involved in instance-specific behavior, if the type of Stream can change at runtime, or it may be sharing the implementation of Stream with all the other users.

A common twist on delegation is to pass the delegator as a parameter to a delegated method.

GraphicEditor
```
public void mouseDown() {
  tool.mouseDown(this);
}
```

RectangleTool
```
public void mouseDown(GraphicEditor editor) {
  editor.add(new RectangleFigure());
}
```

If a delegate needs to send a message to itself, "itself" is ambiguous. Sometimes the message should be sent to the delegating object. Sometimes the message should be sent to the delegate. In the example below the RectangleTool adds a figure, but to the delegating GraphicsEditor, not to itself. The GraphicsEditor could have been passed as a parameter to the delegated mouseDown() method, but in this case it seemed simpler to store a permanent back-reference in the tool. Passing the GraphicsEditor as a parameter makes it possible to use the same tool in multiple editors, but if this isn't important the code with the backpointer may be simpler.

GraphicEditor
```
public void mouseDown() {
  tool.mouseDown();
}
```

RectangleTool
```
private GraphicEditor editor;
public RectangleTool(GraphicEditor editor) {
  this.editor= editor;
}
public void mouseDown() {
  editor.add(new RectangleFigure());
}
```

Pluggable Selector

Let's say you need instance-specific behavior, but only for one or two methods, and you don't mind having all the variants of the code live in one class. In this case, store the name of the method to be invoked in a field and invoke the method by reflection.

Originally, each test in JUnit had to be stored in its own class (Figure 5.7). Each subclass only had one method. Classes seemed conceptually heavy as a way to represent a single class.

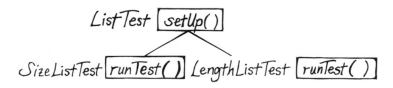

Figure 5.7 *Trivial subclasses to represent different tests*

By implementing a generic runTest(), ListTests with different names run different test methods. The name of the test is assumed to also be the name of a method which is retrieved and run when the test is run. Here is the simple version of the code to implement the pluggable selector version of running a test.

```
String name;
public void runTest() throws Exception {
  Class[] noArguments= new Class[0];
  Method method= getClass().getMethod(name, noArguments);
  method.invoke(this, new Object[0]);
}
```

The simplified class hierarchy uses a single class (Figure 5.8). As with all code compression techniques, the modified code is only easy to read if you understand the "trick".

When pluggable selectors first became widely known, people tended to overuse them. You would be looking at some code, decide it couldn't possibly be called, delete, and have the system break because it was invoked by a pluggable selector somewhere. The costs of using pluggable selectors are considerable, but a limited use to solve a difficult problem may justify the cost.

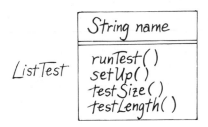

Figure 5.8 *Pluggable selector helps pack tests into a single class*

Anonymous Inner Class

Java offers one more alternative for instance-specific behavior, anonymous inner classes. The idea is to create a class that is only used in one place, that can override one or more methods for strictly local purposes. Because it is only used in one place, the class can be referred to implicitly instead of by name.

Effective use of anonymous inner classes relies on having an extremely simple API—like implementing Runnable with its one method run()—or having a superclass that provides most of the needed implementation so the anonymous inner class can be implemented simply. The code for the anonymous inner class interrupts the presentation of the code in which it is embedded, so it needs to be short so it doesn't distract the reader.

Anonymous inner classes have the limitations that the code to be set in the instance must be known when you write the class (unlike delegates, which can be added later) and it cannot be changed once an instance has been created. Anonymous inner classes are difficult to test directly and so shouldn't contain complicated logic. Because they are un-named, you don't have the opportunity to express your intention for an anonymous inner class with a well-chosen name.

Library Class

Where do you put functionality that doesn't fit into any object? One solution is to create static methods on an otherwise-empty class. No one is expected to ever create instances of this class. It is just there as a holder for the functions in the library.

While library classes are fairly common, they don't scale well. Putting all the logic into static methods forfeits the biggest advantage of programming with objects: a private namespace of shared data that can be used to help simplify logic. Try to turn library classes into objects whenever possible.

Sometimes this is as simple as finding a better home for a method. The Collections library class, for example, has a method sort(List). Such a specific parameter is a hint that this method probably belongs on List instead.

An incremental way to convert a library class to an object is to convert the static methods to instance methods. Maintain the same interface at first by having the static method delegate to an instance method. In a class called Library, for example,

```
public static void method(...params...) {
  ...some logic...
}
```

becomes:

```
public static void method(...params...) {
  new Library().instanceMethod(...params...);
}
private void instanceMethod(...params...) {
  ...some logic...
}
```

Now, if several of the methods have similar parameter lists (and if they don't then the methods probably belong in different classes), convert the method parameters to constructor parameters:

```
public static void method(...params...) {
  new Library(...params...).instanceMethod();
}
private void instanceMethod() {
  ...some logic...
}
```

Next change the interface by moving instance creation to the clients and eliminating the static methods.

```
public void instanceMethod(...params...) {
  ...some logic...
}
```

This experience may give you ideas for how to rename the class and methods so client code reads clearly.

Conclusion

A class bundles together related state. The next chapter presents patterns that communicate decisions about state.

Chapter 6

State

The patterns in this chapter describe how to communicate your use of state. Objects are convenient packages of *behavior* which is presented to the outside world and *state* which is used to support that behavior. One of the advantages of objects is that they mince all of the state of a program into tiny pieces, each effectively its own little computer. Large libraries of state, promiscuously referenced, make further changes to code difficult because the effect of a code change on the state is hard to predict. With objects, it is easier to analyze what state will be affected by a change, because the namespace of referenceable state is so much smaller.

The chapter contains the following patterns:

- State—Compute with values that change over time.

- Access—Maintain flexibility by limiting access to state.

- Direct Access—Directly access state inside an object.

- Indirect Access—Access state through a method to provide greater flexibility.

- Common State—Store the state common to all objects of a class as fields.

- Variable State—Store state whose presence differs from instance to instance as a map.

- Extrinsic State—Store special-purpose state associated with an object in a map held by the user of that state.

- Variable—Variables provide a namespace for accessing state.

- Local Variable—Local variables hold state for a single scope.

- Field—Fields store state for the life of an object.

- Parameter—Parameters communicate state during the activation of a single method.

- Collecting Parameter—Pass a parameter to collect complicated results from multiple methods.

- Parameter Object—Consolidate frequently used long parameter lists into an object.

- Constant—Store state that doesn't vary as a constant.

- Role-Suggesting Name—Name variables after the role they play in a computation.

- Declared Type—Declare a general type for variables.

- Initialization—Initialize variables declaratively as much as possible.

- Eager Initialization—Initialize fields at instance creation time.

- Lazy Initialization—Initialize fields whose values are expensive to calculate just before they are first used.

State

The world persists. If a minute ago the sun was high in the sky, you can be sure it is still high in the sky, but moved a bit. If I cared to calculate, I could predict its new position based on my previous observation, knowledge of the earth's rotation, and measurement of the passage of time.

Thinking of the world as things that change has proven useful for a long time. The Native Americans in the area where I live watched Mt. McLaughlin in the spring. When the snow melted sufficiently that the outline of a flying eagle appeared in the remaining snow, it was time to move down to the Rogue River to catch the spring run of salmon. The state of the snow on the mountain was a valuable clue to the presence of a yummy meal swimming in the water some distance away.

When computing pioneers picked metaphors for programming computers, they latched onto this idea of state changing over time. The human brain has a wide variety of strategies, built-in and learned, for dealing with state.

However, state also poses problems for programmers. As soon as you assume what some bit of state is, your code is at risk. You might assume incorrectly or the state might change. Many desirable programming tools, like automated refactorers, are easier to construct if there is no notion of state.

Finally, concurrency and state don't play well together. Many of the problems of parallel programs vanish if there is no state.

Functional programming languages dispense altogether with changing state. None of these has ever become popular. I think state is a valuable metaphor for us since our brains are structured and conditioned to deal with changing state. Single assignment or variableless programming forces us to discard too many effective thinking strategies to be an attractive choice.

Object languages are a coping strategy for dealing with state. They offer the opportunity to avoid the problem of state changing "behind your back" by partitioning the state in the system into discrete little chunks, each of which has strictly limited access to the others. It is easier to keep track of a handful of bytes than mega- or gigabytes. The problem of incorrectly assuming the value of some state remains, but with objects you have the chance to quickly and accurately review all access to a variable.

A key to managing state effectively is putting similar state together and making sure different state stays apart. Two clues that two bits of state are similar are if the two bits are used in the same computation and if the two bits live and die at the same time. If two pieces of state are used together and have the same lifetime, then having them close to each other is probably a good idea.

Access

One dichotomy in programming languages is the distinction between accessing stored values and invoking computations. The two concepts are understandable in terms of each other. Accessing memory is like invoking a function that returns the currently stored values. Invoking a function is like reading a memory location, the contents of which just happen to be computed and not simply returned. Nevertheless, our programming languages separate invoking computation and accessing memory, so we need to be able to communicate effectively about the difference.

Deciding what to store and what to compute affects the readability, flexibility, and performance of programs. Sometimes these goals conflict with each other and with your programming preference. Sometimes the context changes so that yesterday's reasonable partition between stored and computed no longer makes sense. Making workable decisions today and maintaining the flexibility to change your mind in the future is a key to good software development. It is that need for future change that makes it important for you to communicate your store-versus-compute decisions clearly.

One of the goals of objects was to manage storage. Each object acts as its own little computer with its own memory, isolated to some degree from the other little computers. Current languages, including Java, blur the boundaries between objects by offering public fields. Ease of inter-object access isn't worth the loss of independence between objects.

Direct Access

The simplest way to say "I'm fetching data" or "I'm storing data" is to use direct variable access:

```
x= 10;
```

Direct variable access has the advantage of clarity of expression. When I read x= 10;, I know exactly what is going to happen. This clarity comes with a loss of flexibility. If I store a value in a variable, that's all I can do. If I store values into that variable from many parts of the program, then to make a change I will likely have to change all those parts of the program.

The other downside of direct access is that it is an implementation detail, below the level of most of my thoughts while programming. Setting a variable to 1 may cause my garage door to open, but code that reflects this implementation detail won't communicate well. Compare:

```
doorRegister= 1;
```

with:

```
openDoor();
```

or, with objects:

```
door.open();
```

Most of the thoughts I think while programming have nothing to do with storage. Widespread direct access clutters communication. For those parts of the program where I really am thinking about what is stored where, I use direct access to communicate those thoughts. Storage decisions play a different role for different programmers, so there is no one policy for using direct access that will fit everyone. People keep trying to formulate such rules: direct access only inside accessor methods, and maybe inside constructors too; direct access only inside a single class or inside a class and all its subclasses, or maybe inside an entire package. There is no universal rule. Programmers need to think, communicate, and learn. That's part of being professional.

Indirect Access

You can hide accesses and changes to state behind method invocations. These accessor methods provide flexibility at the cost of clarity and directness. Clients no longer assume that a certain value is stored directly. Thus, you are able to change your mind about storage decisions without affecting client code.

My default strategy for accessing state is to allow direct access inside of a class (including inner classes) and indirect access for clients. This strategy has the advantage that it allows clear, direct access to state for most accesses. Note: if most accesses to an object's state are outside the object, there is a deeper design problem lurking.

Another strategy is to use indirect access exclusively. I find this results in a loss of clarity. Most getting and setting methods are trivial. They often outnumber methods that perform useful work, making the code hard to read. All those getting and setting methods are mighty tempting too. Rather than figure out where a calculation belongs, it is often expedient to implement it wherever and use the accessor methods to deliver the necessary state to make it work.

One definite case for indirect access is where two pieces of data are coupled. Sometimes this coupling is very direct, as in a cached value:

```
Rectangle void setWidth(int width) {
  this.width= width;
  area= width * height;
}
```

Other times the coupling is less direct, through a listener:

```
Widget void setBorder(int width) {
  this.width= width;
  notifyListeners();
}
```

Such coupling is unattractive (it is easy to forget to maintain the implied constraints) but may be the best available option. In such a case, indirect access is best.

Common State

Many calculations share the same data elements even if the values are different. When you find such a calculation, communicate it by declaring fields in a class. For example, all calculations with cartesian points require an abscissa and ordinate. Since all cartesian points share the need for these values, they are most clearly expressed as fields:

```
class Point {
  int x;
  int y;
}
```

Contrast this technique with variable state, where objects of the same class potentially have different data elements. The advantage of common state is that it is clear from reading the code, either the fields themselves or the complete constructor, what data is necessary to have a well-formed object. Your reader will want to know what it takes to successfully invoke the functionality in your object. Common state communicates this clearly and precisely.

Common state in an object should all have the same scope and lifetime. Sometimes I am tempted to introduce a field that is only used by a subset of the methods in an object, or that is only valid while one method is being computed. In such cases I can invariably improve my code by finding somewhere else to store the data in question, perhaps a parameter or a helper object.

Variable State

Sometimes the same object needs different data elements depending on how it is used. It's not just the values that differ; whole different elements are present in objects of the same class.

Variable state is often stored as a map whose keys are the names of the elements (represented as strings or enumerations) and whose values are the data values.

```
class FlexibleObject {
  Map<String, Object> properties= new HashMap<String, Object>();
  Object getProperty(String key) {
    return properties.get(key);
  }
  void setProperty(String key, Object value) {
    properties.set(key, value);
  }
}
```

Variable state is much more flexible than common state. Its primary failing is that it doesn't communicate well. What data elements need to be present for an object with only variable state to function correctly? Only a careful reading of the code and perhaps watching execution will help you answer this question.

I have read code where the programmer overused variable state. Every object of a given class had exactly the same keys in its property map. It would have been much easier for me to read had the same information appeared as field declarations.

One case where variable state seems justified is where the state of one field implies the need for other fields. For example, if I have a widget whose bordered flag is true, then I can also have borderWidth and borderColor. I could communicate this with variable state, as in the design on the top of Figure 6.1.

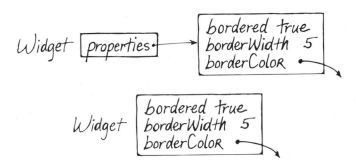

Figure 6.1 *Border represented by variable state and common state*

Common state can also communicate this, as in the bottom of Figure 6.1.

The common state solution violates the principle that all variables in an object should have the same lifetime. Polymorphism provides a clearer explanation of the situation. One class represents the unbordered state and another the bordered state. Bordered has common state to represent its parameters.

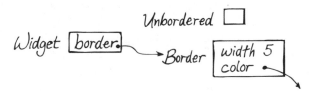

Figure 6.2 *A helper object cleans up the design*

The presence of several variables that share a common prefix is a clue that a helper object of some sort may be useful.

Use common state wherever possible. Use variable state for the fields in an object that may or may not be needed depending on usage.

Extrinsic State

Sometimes a part of your program needs state associated with an object, but the rest of the system doesn't care. For example, information about where an object is stored on disk is useful for the persistence mechanism but not the rest of the code. Putting this data in a field would violate the principle of symmetry. All the rest of the fields are useful for the whole system.

Store special-purpose information associated with an object near where it will be used instead of in the object. In the example above, the persistence mechanism would store an IdentityMap whose keys are the objects stored and whose values are the information about where they are stored.

One weakness of extrinsic state is that it makes copying an object difficult. Replicating an object with extrinsic state isn't as simple as replicating its fields. Instead, all the extrinisic state must also be copied correctly, which could require different handling depending on how that state is used. Another weakness is the difficulty in debugging objects with extrinsic state. A conventional inspector doesn't show all the data associated with an object. Because of these difficulties, extrinsic state is rare but useful when necessary.

Variable

In Java, objects are referred to by variables. Readers need to know about the scope, lifetime, role, and runtime type of variables. While elaborate schemes have been invented to communicate all this information in variable names, simplifying the code using simple names is preferable.

The scope of variables, the extent within which they can be referenced, can be of three types: locals, accessible only within the current scope; fields, which can be accessed anywhere within an object; or static, which can be accessed by any object of a given class. Scope of fields can be extended by the modifiers public, package (the default, and an odd choice for a default since it is the least used), protected, and private.

If you make liberal use of all the combinations available, then it is important to readers that you make the distinctions clear at the point of reference by encoding them in the name. However, to reduce coupling you should mostly use locals and fields with only an occasional static field and the private modifier. By using this limited set of the possible combinations, context suffices to tell the reader whether he is looking at a local or a field. If he can see the declaration the variable is a local, and if he can't then it is a field. This eliminates the need to include scope information in the variable's name. In return you have code with uniform, easily read variable names. All of this presupposes that you can break your code up into small chunks, a property that you can accomplish by applying the other implementation patterns, most notably composed methods.

The lifetime of variables can be smaller than their scope. A field could only be valid while a certain method is active on the stack. That would be ugly. Work hard to ensure that the lifetime of variables is close to their scope. Additionally, make sure that sibling variables (those defined in the same scope) all have the same lifetime.

The type of a variable is adequately communicated through the type declaration. Make sure the declared type communicates as clearly as possible (see "Declared Type"). The one exception to this advice is that the names of variables that hold multiple values (those containing a collection) should be plural. The difference between a single value and multiple values is important for readers.

With scope, lifetime, and type adequately communicated in other ways, the name can be used to convey the role of the variable in the computation. By reducing the information to be conveyed to a minimum, you are free to choose simple names that read well.

Local Variable

Local variables are only accessible from their point of declaration to the end of their scope. Following the principle that information should spread as little as possible, declare local variables just before they are used and in the innermost possible scope.

There are a handful of common roles for local variables:

- Collector: a variable that collects information for later use. Often the contents of collectors are returned as the value of a function. When a collector will be returned, name it `result` or `results`.

- Count: a special collector that collects the count of some other objects.

- Explaining: if you have a complicated expression, assigning bits of the expression to local variables can help readers navigate the complexity:

```
int top= ...;
int left= ...
int height= ...;
int bottom= ...;
return new Rectangle(top, left, height, width);
```

While not computationally necessary, the explaining local variables help what would otherwise be a long, complicated expression.

Explaining locals are often a step towards helper methods. The expression becomes the body of the method, and the name of the local variable suggests a name for the method. Sometimes these helpers are introduced to simplify the calling method. Sometimes they help eliminate the duplication of common expressions.

- Reuse: when an expression's value changes but you need to use the same value more than once, store the value in a local variable. For example, if you need the same timestamp for several objects, you can't fetch the time fresh for each object:

```
for (Clock each: getClocks())
    each.setTime(System.currentTimeMillis());
```

Instead, a reusing local variable freezes time for your purposes:

```
long now= System.currentTimeMillis();
for (Clock each: getClocks())
    each.setTime(now);
```

- Element: the final common use of local variables is to hold the elements of a collection that is being iterated. As in the example above, each is a clear, simple name for an element local variable. If I want to know "each what?" I can glance at the for statement above.

For nested loops, append the name of the collection to the element local name to distinguish them:

```
broadcast() {
    for (Source eachSender: getSenders())
        for (Destination eachReceiver: getReceivers())
            ...;
}
```

Field

The scope and lifetime of a field is the same as the object to which it is attached. Because the primary allegiance of fields is to the object as a whole, declare fields together either at the beginning or end of the class. At the beginning, the declarations give a reader important context to use while reading the rest of the code. Leaving the declarations until last sends the message, "Behavior is king; data is an implementation detail." While I agree philosophically with the statement that logic is more important than data in object programs, I still like to read the declarations first, wherever they are, when I am reading code.

One of your options with a field is to declare it final. This tells readers that the value of the field will not change after the constructor has run. While I mentally keep track of which of my fields are final and which are not, I don't declare fields explicitly. The extra clarity is not worth the extra complexity for me, but if I were writing code that would be changed by many people over a long time, it seems worth making the distinction between final and volatile fields explicit.

The list of roles for fields is not as comprehensive as the list for local variables. However, here are a few common roles for fields:

- Helper: helper fields hold references to objects used by many of an object's methods. If an object is passed as a parameter to many methods, consider replacing the parameter with a helper field set in the complete constructor.

- Flag: boolean flag fields say, "This object can act in two different ways." If there is a setter method for the flag, it additionally says, "... and the behavior can change during the life of the object." Flag fields are fine if they are only used in a few conditionals. If the code making decisions on the basis of the flag is duplicated, consider changing to a strategy field instead.

- Strategy: when you want to express that there are alternative ways to perform some part of an object's computation, store in a field an object performing just the variable part of the computation. If this variation in behavior doesn't change during an object's lifetime, set the strategy field in the complete constructor. Otherwise, provide methods for changing it.

- State: state fields are like strategy fields in that part of the behavior of the object is delegated to them. However, state fields, when triggered, set the following state themselves. Strategy fields are changed, if at all, by other objects. State machines implemented this way can be difficult to read, since the states and transitions are not expressed in one place. However, for simple state machines they can suffice.

- Components: these fields hold objects or data "owned" by the referring object.

Parameter

Besides non-private variables (fields or static fields), the only way to communicate state from one object to another is through parameters. Because non-private variables introduce strong coupling between classes and because that coupling tends to grow over time, parameters are preferable in all cases where both static fields and parameters are possible.

The coupling introduced by a parameter is weaker than the coupling introduced by a permanent reference from one object to another. For example, calculations in the interior of a tree structure sometimes need the parent of a node. Rather than have a permanent reference to the parent (Figure 6.3), passing a parameter to those methods requiring it weakens the coupling between the nodes. With no permanent reference to a parent, it is possible, for example, to have a subtree as part of several trees.

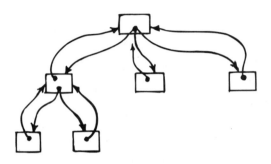

Figure 6.3   *Highly coupled tree structure with parent pointers*

If many messages from one object to another require the same parameter, it may be better to permanently attach the parameter to the called object. Parameters are thin threads tying the object together, but, like Gulliver with the Lilliputians, enough thin threads can render an object incapable of being changed.

Figure 6.4 shows a single parameter.

Figure 6.4   *A single parameter introduces little coupling*

Illustrated with code:

```
Server s= new Server();
s.a(this);
```

Repeating the same parameter five times increases the coupling substantially:

```
Server s= new Server();
s.a(this);
s.b(this);
s.c(this);
s.d(this);
s.e(this);
```

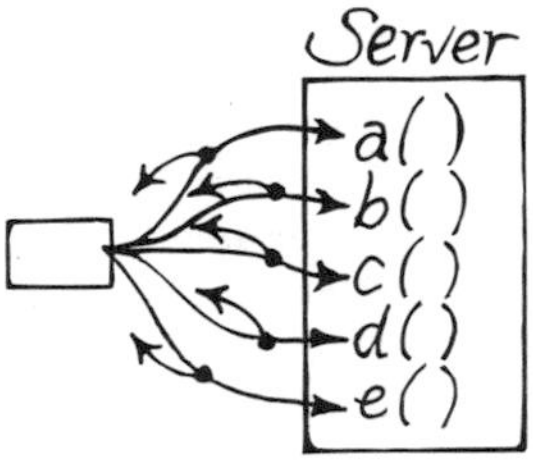

Figure 6.5   *Repeated parameter increases coupling*

In this case, the two objects are better prepared to operate independently if the parameters are replaced by a pointer:

```
Server s= new Server(this);
s.a();
s.b();
s.c();
s.d();
s.e();
```

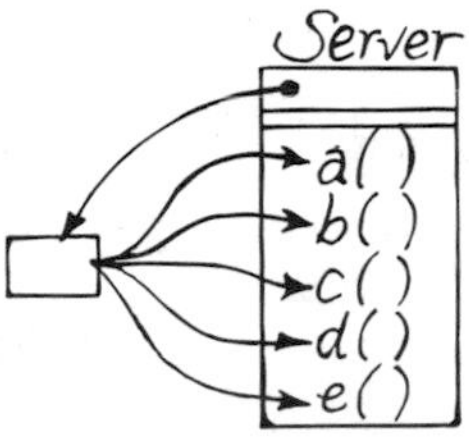

Figure 6.6   *Reference reduces coupling*

Collecting Parameter

Calculations that gather results from many method invocations need some way to merge those results. One way is to return a value from all of the methods. This works if the value is simple, like an integer.

```
Node
int size() {
  int result= 1;
  for (Node each: getChildren())
    result+= each.size();
  return result;
}
```

When merging the results is more complicated than simple addition, it is more direct to pass a parameter that will collect the results. For example, a collecting parameter helps when linearizing a tree:

```
Node
asList() {
  List results= new ArrayList();
  addTo(results);
  return results;
}
addTo(List elements) {
  elements.add(getValue());
  for (Node each: getChildren())
    each.addTo(elements);
}
```

Some other examples of more-complicated collecting parameters are the GraphicsContext that is passed around a tree of widgets or the TestResult that is passed around a tree of tests in JUnit.

Optional Parameter

Some methods can take a parameter or supply a default parameter if one isn't present. In such cases put the mandatory parameters first in the parameter list and add the optional parameters at the end. This makes as many of the parameters as possible the same, and the optional parameters appear as alternatives at the end.

The ServerSocket constructors demonstrate optional parameters. The basic constructor takes no arguments, but there is also a version with an optional port number and another version with an optional port number and an optional backlog length:

```
public ServerSocket()
public ServerSocket(int port)
public ServerSocket(int port, int backlog)
```

Languages with keyword parameters can express optional parameters more directly. Since Java has only positional parameters, whether a parameter is optional can only be expressed by convention. Some people call this the telescoping parameter pattern to provide a physical analogy for how the collection of parameters builds on each other.

Var Args

Some methods can take any number of a given type of parameter. A simple solution is to always pass a collection as the parameter. Callers of such methods, however, are cluttered by the presence of the intermediate collections:

```
Collection<String> keys= new ArrayList<String>();
keys.add(key1);
keys.add(key2);
object.index(keys);
```

This problem is common enough that Java provides a mechanism to pass a variable number of arguments to a method. By declaring the method above as `method(Class... classes)`, the client can invoke the method with any number of arguments:

```
object.index(key1, key2);
```

Var args must be the last parameter. If a method has var args and optional arguments as described above, the optional arguments have to go before the var args.

Parameter Object

If a group of parameters is passed together to many methods, consider making an object whose fields are those parameters and passing the object instead. Once you have replaced the long parameter lists with the parameter object, see if there are bits of code using only the fields in the parameter object that you could turn into methods on the parameter object.

For example, it is common in Java graphics libraries to represent rectangles as independent `x`, `y`, `width`, and `height` parameters. Sometimes these four parameters are passed through many layers of method invocation, resulting in code that is longer and more difficult to read than it needs to be.

```
setOuterBounds(x, y, width, height);
setInnerBounds(x + 2, y + 2, width - 4, height - 4);
```

Making the rectangle explicit as an object explains the code better:

```
setOuterBounds(bounds);
setInnerBounds(bounds.expand(-2));
```

The introduction of the parameter object shortens the code, explains its intent, and provides a home for the algorithm for expanding and contracting a rectangle, which otherwise would have to be repeated everywhere it was required (with frequent errors when programmers forgot that the expansion factor has to be doubled for the width and height). Many powerful objects begin life as parameter objects.

While the primary motivation for introducing a parameter object is to improve readability, parameter objects can become important homes for logic. The fact that the data appears together in several parameter lists is a blatant clue that they are strongly related. A class with its fixed list of fields is an explicit way of communicating "This set of data is strong related."

The argument most often used against parameter objects is performance—allocating all those parameter objects takes time. In most cases this will not be a problem in practice. If object allocation becomes a bottleneck, the parameter object can be inlined, turned back into the explicit list of parameters, where necessary. The best code to optimize is readable, factored, and tested; parameter objects can contribute to these goals.

Constant

Sometimes you have data values that are needed several places within your program but which don't change. If these values are known at compile time, store in variables declared static final and reference the variable throughout your program. It is common to give constants names consisting entirely of upper-case characters, to emphasize that they are not ordinary variables.

Part of the importance of using constants is that you avoid a whole class of errors when using them. If you have 5 embedded throughout your code and you decide to change 5 to 6, it is easy to miss an incidence. If 5 takes on two implicit meanings, say "draw a border" and "what follows is an acknowledgment packet", then changing the constant is even more error-prone. The strongest reason to use constants, though, is because you can use the names of the constants to communicate what you mean by the value. Readers will be able to understand Color.WHITE much better than 0xFFFFFF. If the encoding of color changes, code using the constant will not need to be changed.

A common use of constants is to communicate variations of a message in an interface. For example, to center text you could invoke setJustification(Justification.CENTERED). One advantage of this style of API is that you can add new variants of existing methods by adding new constants without breaking implementors. However, these messages don't communicate as well as having a separate method for each variation. In this style, the message above would be justifyCentered(). An interface where all invocations of a method have literal constants as arguments can be improved by giving it separate methods for each constant value.

Role-Suggesting Name

How do you decide what to call a variable? Many conflicting constraints come to bear on this question. I want to communicate my intent fully through my names, which often suggests long names. I'd like the names to be short to simplify code formatting. Names will be read many times for each time they are typed, so the names should be optimized for readability, not ease of typing. Both the way the data in the variable is used and the role that data plays in the computation need to be expressed.

There are several pieces of information I need when I am trying to understand a variable. What is its purpose in the computation? How is the object referred to by the variable used? What is the scope and lifetime of the variable? How widely is the variable referenced?

Many variable naming schemes include type information in the names. Mine doesn't. What is the point of telling the compiler the types of variables over and over if I have to turn around and embed that same information again in the variable names? I can see including type information in variable names in languages that don't do much to prevent type errors, like C. Java provides ample support for avoiding type errors.

If I want to know the type of one of my variables, my IDE gives me quick feedback about it. Using short, composed methods also provides a quick reference to the most commonly used variables, locals and parameters.

Another facet of variables that readers need to understand is the scope of variables. Some variable naming practices encode the scope as a prefix to the name so fCount is a field and lCount is a local. Again, by composing relatively short methods I find that I am seldom confused by the scope of a variable. If I can't see a declaration of the variable here in this method, it is most likely a field (I use other techniques to avoid most static fields).

This leaves the role of the variable as the primary piece of information I try to communicate with my variable names, generally leading to short, clear names. If I have to struggle to find a name, it is generally because I don't understand the computation very well.

There are a few variable names that recur in my code:

- result—stores the object that will be returned from a function

- each—stores the individual elements of a collection while iterating (although I am becoming fond of using the singular form of the collection's name, for example for (Node child: getChildren())).

- count—stores counts

If I have multiple variables that I would like to give the same name, I qualify the name: eachX and eachY or rowCount and columnCount.

I am sometimes tempted to abbreviate words in variable names. This optimizes typing at the expense of reading. Since variables are read many times for each time they are written, this is a false economy. Sometimes I am tempted to use several words for a variable, which makes the variable too long for comfortable typing. When this happens I look at the surrounding context. Why do I need so many words to distinguish this variable's role from the role of other variables? Often this leads me to simplify the design, allowing me to again write short variable names in good conscience.

To summarize, I communicate the role a variable plays through its name. Everything else important about the variable—its lifetime, scope, and type—can generally be communicated through context.

Declared Type

One of the features of Java and other pessimistically typed languages is the need to declare the types of your variables. Since you have to declare the type, you may as well use the declared type as an opportunity to communicate. Pick the declared type that communicates how the variable is to be used, not how it is implemented.

`List<Person> members= new ArrayList<Person>()` tells me that `members` is to be used like a `List`. I expect to see operations invoked like `get()` and `set()`, since what sets `List` apart from `Collection` is indexed access to elements.

When I was first drafting this pattern, I wrote it dogmatically. Then I tried the rigid rule that all variables should be declared as generally as possibly. What I found was that the extra effort to generalize all types was not worth it. Sometimes a variable would be a `List`. Then I would pass it to a method where only `Collection` protocol was used. The inconsistency between the declarations was a bigger problem for readers than the lack of precision in just declaring it as a `List` everywhere it was used. Now I would say it more gently. It is useful to declare variables and methods with a general type where possible. Losing a little precision and generality to maintain consistency is a reasonable trade-off.

The best thing about generalizing declared types is that it opens up options for changing the concrete classes during later modifications. If I declare a variable as an `ArrayList`, I can't easily change it later to a `HashSet` the way I could if I declared it as a `Collection`. In general, the further a decision propagates, the less flexibility you have for future change. To maintain flexibility, allow as little information as possible to spread as narrowly as possible. There is more information in the statement "`members` contains an `ArrayList`" than in the statement "`members` contains a `Collection`".

Focusing on communication is a good heuristic for maintaining flexibility. Declared types are an example of this. When I say that a variable holds a `Collection`, I am speaking precisely. Communicating well provides the best flexibility.

Initialization

Before you can program, you need to know what you can count on. Being able to make accurate assumptions helps you focus on learning what you need to know. One issue about which it is helpful to be able to make assumptions is the state of variables. Initialization is the process of putting variables into a known state before they are used.

There are several issues in initializing variables. One is the desire to make initialization as declarative as possible. If initialization and declaration go together, there is one place to go for answers to questions about the variable. Another issue is performance. Variables that are expensive to initialize may need to be initialized some time after they come into existence. For example, in Eclipse, classes are loaded as late as possible to keep start-up time low.

Listed below are two initialization patterns: eager and lazy.

Eager Initialization

One style of initialization is to initialize a variable as soon as it comes into existence—when it is declared or when the object in which it lives is created (declaration or constructor). One advantage of eager initialization is that you can be assured that the variables are initialized before they are used.

Initialize variables in the declaration if possible. This puts the declared and actual types close together for readers.

```
class Library {
  List<Person> members= new ArrayList<Person>();
  ...
}
```

Initialize fields in the constructor if they can't be initialized in the declaration:

```
class Point {
  int x, y;
  Point(int x, int y) {
    this.x= x;
    this.y= y;
  }
}
```

There is a certain symmetry to initializing all the fields of an object in the same place, either the declarations or the constructor. However, mixing the two styles doesn't seem to cause any confusion as long as the objects are kept to a reasonable size.

Lazy Initialization

Eager initialization works well when you don't mind paying the cost of computing a variable's value when the variable comes into existence. When the computation is expensive and you would like to defer the cost (perhaps because the variable may never be used), create a getter method and initialize the field when the getter is first called:

```
Library.Collection<Person> getMembers() {
  if (members == null)
    members= new ArrayList<Person>();
  return members;
}
```

Lazy initialization used to be a more common technique. Limitation in raw computing power was more often an issue. Lazy initialization is important when computational power is a limited resource. A resource-constrained environment like Eclipse, where start-up must be fast, uses lazy initialization to avoid loading plug-ins until they are about to be used.

A lazily initialized field is harder to read than one initialized eagerly. The reader has to look at least two places before understanding the implementation type of the field. When coding, you are storing information for future readers. Fortunately, there are only a few commonly asked questions, so a few techniques suffice to answer most of them. Lazy initialization says, "Performance is important here."

Conclusion

The state patterns talk about how to communicate decisions about representing the state in a program. The next chapter presents the other side of the coin, how to communicate decisions about the flow of control.

Chapter 7

Behavior

John Von Neumann contributed one of the primary metaphors of computing—a sequence of instructions that are executed one by one. This metaphor permeates most programming languages, Java included. The topic of this chapter is how to express the behavior of a program. The patterns are:

- Control Flow—Express computations as a sequence of steps.

- Main Flow—Clearly express the main flow of control.

- Message—Express control flow by sending a message.

- Choosing Message—Vary the implementors of a message to express choices.

- Double Dispatch—Vary the implementors of messages along two axes to express cascading choices.

- Decomposing Message—Break complicated calculations into cohesive chunks.

- Reversing Message—Make control flows symmetric by sending a sequence of messages to the same receiver.

- Inviting Message—Invite future variation by sending a message that can be implemented in different ways.

- Explaining Message—Send a message to explain the purpose of a clump of logic.

- Exceptional Flow—Express the unusual flows of control as clearly as possible without interfering with the expression of the main flow.

- Guard Clause—Express local exceptional flows by an early return.

- Exception—Express non-local exceptional flows with exceptions.

- Checked Exception—Ensure that exceptions are caught by declaring them explicitly.

- Exception Propagation—Propagate exceptions, transforming them as necessary so the information they contain is appropriate to the catcher.

Control Flow

Why do we have control flow in programs at all? There are languages like Prolog that don't have an explicit notion of a flow of control. Bits of logic float around in a soup, waiting for the right conditions before becoming active.

Java is a member of the family of languages in which the sequence of control is a fundamental organizing principle. Adjacent statements execute one after the other. Conditionals cause code to execute only in certain circumstances. Loops execute code repeatedly. Messages are sent to activate one of several subroutines. Exceptions cause control to jump up the stack.

All of these mechanisms add up to a rich medium for expressing computations. As an author/programmer, you decide whether to express the flow you have in mind as one main flow with exceptions, multiple alternative flows each of which is equally important, or some combination. You group bits of the control flow so they can be understood abstractly at first, for the casual reader, with greater detail available for those who need to understand them. Some groupings are routines in a class, some are by delegating control to another object.

Main Flow

Programmers generally have in mind a main flow of control for their programs. Processing starts here, ends there. There may be decisions and exceptions along the way, but the computation has a path to follow. Use your programming language to clearly express that flow.

Some programs, particularly those that are designed to work reliably in hostile circumstances, don't really have a visible main flow. These programs are in the minority, however. Using the expressive power of your programming language to clearly express little-executed, seldom-changed facts about your program obscures the more highly leveraged part of your program: the part that will be read, understood, and changed frequently. It's not that exceptional conditions are unimportant, just that focusing on expressing the main flow of the computation clearly is more valuable.

Therefore, clearly express the main flow of your program. Use exceptions and guard clauses to express unusual or error conditions.

Message

One of the primary means of expressing logic in Java is the message. Procedural languages use procedure calls as an information hiding mechanism:

```
compute() {
  input();
  process();
  output();
}
```

says, "For purposes of understanding this computation all you need to know is that it consists of these three steps, the details of which are not important at the moment." One of the beauties of programming with objects is that the same procedure also expresses something richer. For every method, there is potentially a whole set of similarly structured computations whose details differ. And, as an extra added bonus, you don't have to nail down the details of all those future variations when you write the invariant part.

Using messages as the fundamental control flow mechanism acknowledges that change is the base state of programs. Every message is a potential place where the receiver of the message can be changed without changing the sender. Rather than saying "There is something out there the details of which aren't important," the message-based version of the procedure says, "At this point in the story something interesting happens around the idea of input. The details may vary." Using this flexibility wisely, making clear and direct expressions of logic where possible and deferring details appropriately, is an important skill if you want to write programs that communicate effectively.

Choosing Message

Sometimes I send a message to choose an implementation, much as a case statement is used in procedural languages. For example, if I am going to display a graphic in one of several ways, I will send a polymorphic message to communicate that a choice will take place at runtime.

```
public void displayShape(Shape subject, Brush brush) {
  brush.display(subject);
}
```

The message display() chooses the implementation based on the runtime type of the brush. Then I am free to implement a variety of brushes: ScreenBrush, PostscriptBrush, and so on.

Liberal use of choosing messages leads to code with few explicit conditionals. Each choosing message is an invitation to later extension. Each explicit conditional is another point in your program that will require explicit modification in order to modify the behavior of the whole program.

Reading code that uses lots of choosing messages requires skill to learn. One of the costs of choosing messages is that a reader may have to look at several classes before understanding the details of a particular path through the computation. As a writer you can help the reader navigate by giving the methods intention-revealing names. Also, be aware of when a choosing message is overkill. If there is no possible variation in a computation, don't introduce a method just to provide the possibility of variation.

Double Dispatch

Choosing messages are good for expressing a single dimension of variability. In the example in "Choosing Message," this dimension was the type of medium on which the shape was to be drawn. If you need to express two independent dimensions of variability, you can cascade two choosing messages.

For example, suppose I wanted to express that a Postscript oval was computed differently than a screen rectangle. First I would decide where I wanted the computations to live. The base computations seeem like they belong in the Brush, so I will send a choosing message first to the Shape, then to the Brush:

```
displayShape(Shape subject, Brush brush) {
  shape.displayWith(brush);
}
```

Now each Shape has the opportunity to implement displayWith() differently. Rather than do any detailed work, however, they append their type onto the message and defer to the Brush:

```
Oval.displayWith(Brush brush) {
  brush.displayOval(this);
}
Rectangle.displayWith(Brush brush) {
  brush.displayRectangle(this);
}
```

Now the different kinds of brushes have the information they need to do their work:

```
PostscriptBrush.displayRectangle(Rectangle subject) {
  writer print(subject.left() +" " +...+ " rect);
}
```

Double dispatch introduces some duplication with a corresponding loss of flexibility. The type names of the receivers of the first choosing message get scattered over the methods in the receiver of the second choosing message. In this example, this means that to add a new Shape, I would have to add methods to all the Brushes. If one dimension is more likely to change than the other, make it the receiver of the second choosing message.

The computer scientist in me wants to generalize to triple, quadruple, quintuple dispatch. However, I've only ever attempted triple dispatch once and it didn't stay for long. I have always found clearer ways to express multi-dimensional logic.

Decomposing (Sequencing) Message

When you have a complicated algorithm composed of many steps, sometimes you can group related steps and send a message to invoke them. The intended purpose of the message isn't to provide a hook for specialization or anything sophisticated like that. It is just old-fashioned functional decomposition. The message is there simply to invoke the sub-sequence of steps in the routine.

Decomposing messages need to be descriptively named. Most readers should be able to gather what they need to know about the purpose of the sub-sequence from the name alone. Only those readers interested in implementation details should have to read the code invoked by the decomposing message.

Difficulty naming a decomposing message is a tip-off that this isn't the right pattern to use. Another tip-off is long parameter lists. If I see these symptoms, I inline the method invoked by the decomposing message and apply a different pattern, like Method Object, to help me communicate the structure of the program.

Reversing Message

Symmetry can improve the readability of code. Consider the following code:

```
void compute() {
  input();
  helper.process(this);
  output();
}
```

While this method is composed of three others, it lacks symmetry. The readability of the method is improved by introducing a helper method that reveals the latent symmetry. Now when reading compute(), I don't have to keep track of who is sent the messages—they all go to this.

```
void process(Helper helper) {
  helper.process(this);
}
void compute() {
  input();
  process(helper);
  output();
}
```

Now the reader can understand how the compute() method is structured by reading a single class.

Sometimes the helper method invoked by a reversing message becomes important on its own. Sometimes, overuse of reversing messages can obscure the need to move functionality. If we had the following code:

```
void input(Helper helper) {
  helper.input(this);
}
void output(Helper helper) {
  helper.output(this);
}
```

it would probably be better structured by moving the whole compute() method to the Helper class:

```
compute() {
  new Helper(this).compute();
}
Helper.compute() {
  input();
  process();
  output();
}
```

Sometimes I feel silly introducing methods "just" to satisfy an "aesthetic" urge like symmetry. Aesthetics go deeper than that. Aesthetics engage more of your brain than strictly linear logical thought. Once you have cultivated your sense of the aesthetics of code, the aesthetic impressions you receive of your code is valuable feedback about the quality of the code. Those feelings that bubble up from below the surface of symbolic thought can be as valuable as your explicitly named and justified patterns.

Inviting Message

Sometimes as you are writing code, you expect that people will want to vary a part of the computation in a subclass. Send an appropriately named message to communicate the possibility of later refinement. The message invites programmers to refine the computation for their own purposes later.

If there is a default implementation of the logic, make it the implementation of the message. If not, declare the method abstract to make the invitation explicit.

Explaining Message

The distinction between intention and implementation has always been important in software development. It is what allows you to understand a computation first in essence and later, if necessary, in detail. You can use messages to make this distinction by sending a message named after the problem you are solving which in turn sends a message named after how the problem is to be solved.

The first example I saw of this was in Smalltalk. Transliterated, the method that caught my eye was this:

```
highlight(Rectangle area) {
  reverse(area);
}
```

I thought, "Why is this useful? Why not just call reverse() directly instead of calling the intermediate highlight() method?" After some thought, though, I realized that while highlight() didn't have a computational purpose, it did serve to communicate an intention. Calling code could be written in terms of what problem they were trying to solve, namely highlighting an area of the screen.

Consider introducing an explaining message when you are tempted to comment a single line of code. When I see:

```
flags |= LOADED_BIT; // Set the loaded bit
```

I would rather read:

```
setLoadedFlag();
```

Even though the implementation of setLoadedFlag() is trivial. The one-line method is there to communicate.

```
void setLoadedFlag() {
  flags |= LOADED_BIT;
}
```

Sometimes the helper methods invoked by explaining messages become valuable points for further extension. It's nice to get lucky when you can. However, my main purpose in invoking an explaining message is to communicate my intention more clearly.

Exceptional Flow

Just as programs have a main flow, they can also have one or more exceptional flows. These are paths of computation that are less important to communicate because they are less-frequently executed, less-frequently changed, or conceptually less important than the main flow. Express the main flow clearly, and these exceptional paths as clearly as possible without obscuring the main flow. Guard clauses and exceptions are two ways of expressing exceptional flows.

Programs are easiest to read if the statements execute one after another. Readers can use comfortable and familiar prose-reading skills to understand the intent of the program. Sometimes, though, there are multiple paths through a program. Expressing all paths equally would result in a bowl of worms, with flags set *here* and used *there* and return values with special meanings. Answering the basic question, "What statements are executed?" becomes an exercise in a combination of archaeology and logic. Pick the main flow. Express it clearly. Use exceptions to express other paths.

Guard Clause

While programs have a main flow, some situations require deviations from the main flow. The guard clause is a way to express simple and local exceptional situations with purely local consequences. Compare the following:

```
void initialize() {
  if (!isInitialized()) {
    ...
  }
}
```

with:

```
void initialize() {
  if (isInitialized())
    return;
  ...
}
```

When I read the first version, I make a note to look for an else clause while I am reading the then clause. I mentally put the condition on a stack. All of this is a distraction while I am reading the body of the then clause. The first two lines of the second version simply give me a fact to note: the receiver hasn't been initialized.

If-then-else expresses alternative, equally important control flows. A guard clause is appropriate for expressing a different situation, one in which one of the control flows is more important than the other. In the initialization example above, the important control flow is what happens when the object is initialized. Other than that, there is just a simple fact to notice, that even if an object is asked to initialize multiple times it will only execute the initialization code once.

Back in the old days of programming, a commandment was issued: each routine shall have a single entry and a single exit. This was to prevent the confusion possible when jumping into and out of many locations in the same routine. It made good sense when applied to FORTRAN or assembly language programs written with lots of global data where even understanding which statements were executed was hard work. In Java, with small methods and mostly local data, it is needlessly conservative. However, this bit of programming folklore, thoughtlessly obeyed, prevents the use of guard clauses.

Guard clauses are particularly useful when there are multiple conditions:

```java
void compute() {
  Server server= getServer();
  if (server != null) {
    Client client= server.getClient();
    if (client != null) {
      Request current= client.getRequest();
      if (current != null)
        processRequest(current);
    }
  }
}
```

Nested conditionals breed defects. The guard clause version of the same code notes the prerequisites to processing a request without complex control structures:

```java
void compute() {
  Server server= getServer();
  if (server == null)
    return;
  Client client= server.getClient();
  if (client == null)
    return;
  Request current= client.getRequest();
  if (current == null)
    return;
  processRequest(current);
}
```

A variant of guard clause is the continue statement used in a loop. It says, "Never mind this element. Go on to the next one."

```
while (line = reader.readline()) {
  if (line.startsWith('#') || line.isEmpty())
    continue;
  // Normal processing here
}
```

Again, the intent is to point out the (strictly local) difference between normal and exceptional processing.

Exception

Exceptions are useful for expressing jumps in program flow that span levels of function invocation. If you realize many levels up on the stack that a problem has occurred—a disk is full or a network connection has been lost—you may only be able to reasonably deal with that fact much lower down on the call stack. Throwing an exception at the point of discovery and catching at the point where it can be handled is much better than cluttering all the intervening code with explicit checks for all the possible exceptional conditions, none of which can be handled.

Exceptions cost. They are a form of design leakage. The fact that the called method throws an exception influences the design and implementation of all possible calling methods until the method is reached that catches the exception. They make it difficult to trace the flow of control, since adjacent statements can be in different methods, objects, or packages. Code that could be written with conditionals and messages, but is implemented with exceptions, is fiendishly difficult to read as you are forever trying to figure out what more is going on than a simple control structure. In short, express control flows with sequence, messages, iteration, and conditionals (in that order) wherever possible. Use exceptions when not doing so would confuse the simply communicated main flow.

Checked Exceptions

One of the dangers of exceptions is what happens if you throw an exception but no one catches it. The program terminates, that's what happens. But you'd like to control when the program terminates unexpectedly, printing out information necessary to diagnose the situation and telling the user what has happened.

Exceptions that are thrown but not caught are an even bigger risk when different people write the code that throws the exception and the code that catches the exception. Any missed communication results in an abrupt and impolite program termination.

To avoid this situation, Java has checked exceptions. These are declared explicitly by the programmer and checked by the compiler. Code that is subject to having a checked exception thrown at it must either catch the exception or pass it along.

Checked exceptions come with considerable costs. First is the cost of the declarations themselves. These can easily add 50% to the length of method declarations and add another thing to read and understand along the levels between the thrower and catcher. Checked exceptions also make changing code more difficult. Refactoring code with checked exceptions is more difficult and tedious than code without, even though modern IDEs reduce the burden.

Exception Propagation

Exceptions occur at different levels of abstraction. Catching and reporting a low-level exception can be confusing to someone who is not expecting it. When a web server shows me an error page with stack trace headed by a `NullPointerException`, I'm not sure what I'm supposed to do with the information. I'd rather see a message that said, "The programmer did not consider the scenario you have just presented." I wouldn't mind if the page also provided a pointer to further information that I could send to a programmer so he could diagnose the problem, but presenting me with untranslated details isn't helpful.

Low-level exceptions often contain valuable information for diagnosing a defect. Wrap the low-level exception in the higher-level exception so that when the exception is printed, on a log for example, enough information is written to help find the defect.

Conclusion

Control flows between methods of a program built from objects. The next chapter describes using methods to express the concepts in a computation.

Chapter 8

Methods

Logic is divided into methods, not smooshed together in one big lump. Why? What problems can be solved by introducing a new one of those pieces? What is the point of having methods at all? Conceptually, at least, you could organize any program as one gigantic routine with control jumping every which way. While this was how early programs were structured (with occasional recent reversions), the big-lump-of-logic suffers from problems. The most serious is that it is difficult to read. With one giant routine it is difficult to distinguish important parts from less important parts. It is difficult to understand part of the program now and leave some details for later. It is difficult to separate what is important for invokers of some functionality from what is important for those who need to modify that functionality. The second problem is that most problems encountered during programming are not unique. Rather than implement everything from scratch each time, it is handy (and productive) to be able to simply invoke a previous solution. The gigantic routine provides no handy way to refer to parts for later reuse.

Dividing the logic of a program into methods gives you a way to say, "These bits of logic aren't closely connected." Dividing the methods into classes and the classes into packages carries this communication further. Putting this code in this method and that code in that method signals readers that the two bits of code aren't intimately related. They can be read and understood separately. Furthermore, the naming of methods gives you a chance to communicate to the reader what the purpose of this bit of the computation is, regardless of its implementation. Readers can often glean what they need from reading the names of methods alone.

Methods also neatly solve the reuse problem. When you are writing a new routine and you need a bit of logic that already exists as a method, you can invoke that method.

Dividing a large computation into methods is conceptually simple: put the pieces that go together together and the pieces that go apart apart. In practice, though, you will spend time, energy, and creativity first figuring out what goes together and what doesn't, and second figuring out how best to make the division. What is a good division in the moment may not work when you change the logic of the system later on. The divisions need to be ones that simplify your overall workload. Knowing which division will work best comes through experience. Here are some of my hints from my experience.

The common issues in dividing a program into methods are the size, purpose, and naming of the methods. If you make too many too small methods, readers will have a hard time following your fragmented expression of ideas. Too few methods leads to duplication and the attendant loss of flexibility. There are many cliché tasks in programming, and creating a new method is a common step towards accomplishing many of these tasks. Methods that solve one of these recurring problems are generally easy to name. Naming methods that solve unique problems is harder but important for readers.

Here are the method-related patterns:

- Composed Method—Compose methods out of calls to other methods.

- Intention-Revealing Name—Name methods after what they are intended to do.

- Method Visibility—Make methods as private as possible.

- Method Object—Turn complex methods into their own objects.

- Overridden Method—Override methods to express specialization.

- Overloaded Method—Provide alternative interfaces to the same computation.

- Method Return Type—Declare the most general possible return type.

- Method Comment—Comment methods to communicate information not easily read from the code.

- Helper Method—Create small, private methods to express the main computation more succinctly.

- Debug Print Method—Use toString() to print useful debugging information.

- Conversion—Express the conversion of one type of object to another cleanly.

- Conversion Method—For simple, limited conversions, provide a method on the source object that returns the converted object.

- Conversion Constructor—For most conversions, provide a method on the converted object's class that takes the source object as a parameter.

- Creation—Express object creation clearly.

- Complete Constructor—Write constructors that return fully formed objects.

- Factory Method—Express more complex creation as a static method on a class rather than a constructor.

- Internal Factory—Encapsulate in a helper method object creation that may need explanation or later refinement.

- Collection Accessor Method—Provide methods that allow limited access to collections.

- Boolean Setting Method—If it helps communication, provide two methods to set boolean values, one for each state.

- Query Method—Return boolean values with methods named asXXX.

- Equality Method—Define `equals()` and `hashCode()` together.

- Getting Method—Occasionally provide access to fields with a method returning that field.

- Setting Method—Even less frequently provide the ability to set fields with a method.

- Safe Copy—Avoid aliasing errors by copying objects passed in or out of accessor methods.

Composed Method

Compose methods out of calls to other methods, each of which is at roughly the same level of abstraction.

One of the signs of a poorly composed method is a mixture of abstraction levels:

```
void compute() {
  input();
  flags |= 0x0080;
  output();
}
```

Code like this is jarring to the reader. Code is easier to understand when it flows, and abruptly shifting abstraction levels breaks flow. What is that bit twiddling in there? I ask myself when reading the above method. What does it mean?

One objection to the use of lots of little methods is the performance penalty imposed by the invocation of all those methods. As I was writing this I wrote a little benchmark program that compared a million loop iterations with a million messages. The overhead was 20-30% on average, not enough to affect the performance of most programs. The combination of faster CPUs and the strongly localized nature of performance bottlenecks makes code performance an issue best left until you can gather statistics from realistic data sets.

How long should a method be? Some people recommend numerical limits, like less than a page or 5-15 lines. While it may be true that most readable code satisfies such a limit, limits beg the question "why?" Why do chunks of logic work out best when they are about so big?

Code readers need to solve several problems that provide opposing influences on the size of methods. When reading for overall structure, seeing lots of code at once is valuable. The white space in the method provides clues to the overall structure and complexity of the code. Are there conditionals and loops? How deeply nested are the control strucutres? How much work is necessary to accomplish the task implied by the name of the method?

The same big method that helped me orient myself becomes a hindrance when I turn to trying to understand the code in detail. I can only usefully hold one brainful of detail at a time, and a thousand-line method contains way more than one brainful. To understand details, I want closely related details gathered together and segregated from irrelevant details.

Simultaneously supporting browsing and digesting is the challenge of the code author who is dividing logic into methods. I find that my code reads best when I break it into relatively small methods (at least by C standards). The trick is recognizing when I have relatively independent sets of details that can be deferred to supporting methods. Sometimes I have too many details for easy comprehension but that are not easy to partition. In that case I create a method object to give all the details a place to be organized.

Another issue in choosing method size is specialization. Right-sized methods can be overridden whole, without having to copy code down to the subclass and edit it nor having to override two methods for one conceptual change.

Compose methods based on facts, not speculation. Get your code working, then decide how it should be structured. If you spend a lot of time structuring your code beforehand, you'll just have to undo all that work and redo it when you learn something during implementation. When I have all the details of the logic laid out in front of me, it is much easier to compose methods sensibly. Sometimes I think I know how methods should be composed, but when I get the logic divided up I find that the result is hard to read. In such cases I find it helpful to inline all the methods until I have one gigantic method again and re-partition it based on my recent experience.

Intention-Revealing Name

Methods should be named for the purpose a potential invoker might have in mind for using the method. There are other bits of information you might like to convey in the name—implementation strategy, for example. However, communicate intent in the name and communicate other information about the method in other ways.

Implementation strategy is the extraneous information most often included in method names. For example:

```
Customer.linearCustomerSearch(String id)
```

This might seem superior to:

```
Customer.find(String id)
```

because it communicates more about the method. However, the goal as a code author is not to simply blurt out everything you can about your program as quickly as you can. Sometimes, restraint is required. Unless the implementation strategy is relevant to users, leave it out of the name. The curious can look at the body of the method to see how it is implemented. Even if Customer offered both linear and hashed lookup, it would be better to communicate the distinction from the invoker's perspective through the names:

```
Customer.find(String id)
Customer.fastFind(String id)
```

(Actually, in this case it would probably be better to just offer one find() that satisfied all users, but that's a different story.) Whether the fast version of find() is implemented with a hash table or a tree is not really relevant to users of the method.

Think about methods' names based on how they look in calling code. That's where readers are likely to first encounter the name. Why was this method invoked and not some other? That is a question that can profitably be answered by the name of the method. The calling method should be telling a story. Name methods so they help tell the story.

If you are implementing methods by analogy with an existing interface, give your methods the same names as those used in the interface. If you have a special kind of iterator, call your methods hasNext() and next(), even if you don't formally implement the Iterator interface. If your methods are only kind of similar, first think about whether you are using the right metaphor, then express the differences as prefixes to the method name.

Method Visibility

The four levels of visibility—public, package, protected, private—each say something different about your intentions for a method.

The two big conflicting constraints in method visibility are the need to have some functionality revealed to outside users and the need to maintain future flexibility. The more methods that are revealed, the harder it is to change the interface to an object should you need to. In developing JUnit, Erich Gamma and I often disagree about the visibility of methods. My Smalltalk background suggests that making methods visible is potentially valuable to clients. Erich's Eclipse experience has taught him to value the flexibility that comes from revealing as little as possible. I'm slowly coming around to his point of view.

You have two costs to balance in choosing visibility. One is the cost of future flexibility. A very narrow interface makes future changes easier. The other cost is the cost to invoke your object. A too-narrow interface leaves all clients performing more work than necessary to use your object. Balancing these costs is central to making good visibility decisions.

My general strategy for visibility is to restrict it as much as possible. If that were all there was to picking visibility, it would be easy. A tool could assign method visibility. The real challenge comes when you are no longer working with certain knowledge, when code out of your direct control begins invoking your methods. Then you have to speculate, to decide which methods are going to be public or protected, committing you to maintaining them or paying a substantial cost to change them.

- Public: when you declare a method public you are saying that you believe it is useful outside of the package in which it is declared. Making a method public means you accept responsibility for maintaining it, either by leaving it unchanged, by fixing all callers if you change it, or by at least notifying the programmers who call it.

  ```
  public Object next();
  ```

  This declaration says that now and for the foreseeable future, next() will be available to clients.

- Package: package visibility is a statement that this method is useful to objects in this package but you aren't willing to commit to making it available to outside objects. This is a kind of odd statement—other objects need this method, but not all other objects, just mine. Treat package method visibility as a suggestion that either functionality should be moved around so the method can be made less visible or perhaps the method is more widely useful than you suspected and it may be worth the cost of making it public.

- Protected: protected visibility is only useful when offering code to be reused by subclassing. While it seems more restrictive than package visibility, the two are really orthogonal, since subclasses outside the package can see and invoke protected methods.

- Private: private methods are the ultimate in future flexibility since you are guaranteed that you will be able to find and change all callers, whether outsiders use and extend your code or not. By making a method private, you are saying that the value of this method to outsiders is not worth the cost of making it more widely available.

Slowly reveal methods, beginning with the most restrictive visibility that will work and revealing them as necessary. If a method no longer needs to be so visible, reduce its visibility. Reducing visibility only works when you have access to all the callers of your code, so you can be certain that you are not breaking a client by eliminating from view a method they relied on. I often notice that methods that I initially thought of as private become valued members of an interface once I begin using an object in new ways.

Declaring methods final is similar to choosing their visibility. Declaring a method final states that while you don't mind people using this method, you won't allow anyone to change it. If the invariants maintained by the method are complicated and subtle enough, this level of self-protection may be justified. You pay for the assurance that no one will accidentally break your object by eliminating the possibility that someone could profitably override it, and instead will have to do more work to get their job done some other way. I don't use final myself, and I have occasionally been frustrated when encountering final methods when I had a legitimate reason to override a method.

Declaring a method static makes it visible even if the caller does not have access to an instance of the class (subject to modification by the other visibility keywords). Static methods are limited in that they can't rely on any instance state, so they aren't a good repository for complex logic. Static methods can be inherited, but once overridden the superclass method cannot be invoked. One good use of static methods is as a replacement for constructors.

Method Object

This is one of my favorite patterns, probably because I use it so infrequently but the results are spectacular when I do. Creating method object can help you turn a tangled mass of code packed into an impossible method into readable, clear code that gradually reveals details to readers. This is a pattern I apply after I have some code working, and the more complex the method the better.

To create a method object, look for a long method with lots of parameters and temporary variables. Trying to extract any part of the method would result in long parameter lists in difficult-to-name sub-methods. Here are the steps to create a method object (since this refactoring is not yet supported automatically as I write this):

1. Create a class named after the method. For example, `complexCalculation()` becomes `ComplexCalculator`.

2. Create a field in the new class for each parameter, local variable, and field used in the method. Give these fields the same names as they have in the original method (you can fix names later).

3. Create a constructor that takes as parameters the method parameters of the original method and the fields of the original object used by the method.

4. Copy the method into a new method, `calculate()`, in the new class. The parameters, locals, and fields used in the old method become field references in the new object.

5. Replace the body of the original method with code that creates an instance of the new class and invokes `calculate()`. For example:

```
complexCalculation() {
    new ComplexCalculator().calculate();
}
```

6. If fields were set in the original method, set them after `calculate()` returns:

```
complexCalculation() {
    ComplexCalculator calculator= new ComplexCalculator();
    calculator.calculate();
    mean= calculator.mean;
    variance= calculator.variance;
}
```

Make sure the refactored code works just like the old code did. Now the fun begins. The code in the new class is easy to refactor. You can extract methods and never have to pass any parameters because all the data used by the method is stored in fields. Often, once you begin extracting methods you will discover that some variables can be demoted from fields to locals. Similarly, there may be information that can be passed into a single method as a parameter instead of being stored in a field. Once you begin extracting methods, you may find that common sub-expressions that were hard to isolate before become useful helper methods with meaningful names.

Sometimes, by the time I suspect that a method object may be called for, the original method has already been sliced up. In such a case, inline all the sub-methods so you have it all in one place before you begin. A clear indication that you need to do more inlining before making the method object is the need to call methods in the original object. Back up, inline them, and start over.

Overridden Method

One of the beauties of programming with objects is the variety of ways they provide to express the differences between similar calculations. Overridden methods are a clear way to express a variation. Methods declared abstract in a superclass are a clear invitation to specialize a calculation, but any method not declared final is a candidate for expressing a variation on an existing calculation. Well-composed methods in the superclass provide a multitude of potential hooks on which you can hang your own code. If the superclass code is in small, cohesive chunks, then you'll be able to override whole methods.

Overriding a method is not either/or. You can execute the subclass' code and the superclass' code by invoking super.method();. Only do this to invoke the method of the same name. If your subclass explicitly chooses to sometimes invoke its own code and sometimes to invoke the superclass code for a variety of methods, the class will be hard to follow and easy to break accidentally. If you feel the need for invoking different superclass methods, you can improve the code by restructuring the control flow until bouncing back and forth between subclass and superclass is no longer necessary.

Superclass methods that are too large create a dilemma: copy code down to the subclass and edit it or find another way to express the variation? The problem with copying is that someone can come along later and change the superclass code you've copied, breaking your code without you (or them) knowing it.

Overloaded Method

When you declare the same method with different parameter types, you are saying, "Here are alternative formats for the parameters to this method." An example is a method that can take a String representing a file name or an Output-Stream, giving users who want to talk in terms of file names a simple interface but preserving flexibility for those users who want to pass in an already-formed stream (for testing, for example). Overloaded methods relieve the caller of the responsibility of converting parameters if there are several legitimate ways of passing the parameters.

A variant of overloading is using the same method name with different numbers of parameters. The problem with this style of overloading is that readers who want to ask, "What happens when I invoke this method?" need to read not only the name of the method but also the parameter list before they know enough to figure out what happens as a result of the method invocation. If the overloading is complicated, readers need to understand subtle overload resolution rules to be able to statically determine which method will be invoked for given types of arguments.

Overloaded methods should all serve the same purpose, with the variation only in the parameter types. Different return types for different overloaded methods make reading the code too difficult. Better to find a new name for the new intention. Give different computations different names.

Method Return Type

The return type of a method signals first whether the method is a procedure that works by side-effect or a function returning a particular type of object. The magic return type void allows Java to avoid a keyword to distinguish between procedures and functions.

Assuming you are writing a function, pick a return type to express your intention. Sometimes your intention is that the return type is specific, a concrete class or one of the primitive types. However, you'd like your methods to be as broadly applicable as possible, so pick the most abstract return type that expresses your intention. This preserves the flexibility for you to change the concrete return type should that become necessary in the future.

Generalizing the return type can also be a way for you to hide implementation details. For example, returning a Collection instead of a List can encourage users not to assume that elements are in a fixed order.

Return types are a common area for changes as you evolve your program. You may begin by returning a concrete class and then discover later that several related methods return different concrete classes, each of which do or should share a common interface. Expressing this similarity by declaring the common interface (if necessary) and returning the new interface from all the methods will help readers understand the similarity.

Method Comment

Express as much information as possible through the names and structure of the code. Add comments to express information that is not obvious from the code. Where they are expected, add javadoc comments to explain the purpose of methods and classes.

Many comments are completely redundant in code written to communicate. The cost of writing them and maintaining their consistency with the code is not worth the value they bring.

Method comments are at an awkward level of abstraction. If there are constraints between two methods (one must be called before the other, for example), where does the comment go? Comments must be kept up-to-date separately with the code, and there is no immediate feedback when comments are no longer valid.

Automated tests can communicate information that doesn't fit naturally in method comments. In the example above, I can write a test that ensures that the appropriate exception is thrown if the methods are invoked in the wrong order (though I would prefer to eliminate or encapsulate this constraint). Automated tests have many advantages. Writing them is a valuable design exercise, especially when done before implementation. If the tests run, they are consistent with the code. Automated refactoring tools can help keep tests updated at low cost.

All that said, communication is still the paramount value in these implementation patterns. If a method comment is the best possible medium for communication, write a good comment.

Helper Method

Helpers are one consequence of composed methods. If you are going to divide big methods into several smaller ones, you need those smaller methods. These are the helpers. Their purpose is to make larger-scale computations more readable by hiding temporarily irrelevant details and giving you a chance to express your intention through the name of the method. Helpers are typically declared private, moving to protected if the class is intended to be refined by subclassing.

You may create a method as a private helper only to discover that external users wish to invoke it. If the method is useful internally, there is a chance that it will be useful externally as well. Even if your little helper never "graduates", however, it is still valuable as a point of communication.

Helpers tend to be short, but they can be too short. Just today I eliminated a helper that returned only a class' constructor. I find that:

```
return testClass.getConstructor().newInstance();
```

communicates as well as:

```
return getTestConstructor().newInstance();
```

However, that helper method might still be justified if subclasses were overriding how the constructor was computed.

Eliminate helpers (at least temporarily) when the logic of a method becomes unclear. Inline all the helper methods, take a fresh look at the logic, and re-extract methods that make sense.

A final purpose for helper methods is eliminating common sub-expressions. If you call a helper method every place in a class you need a certain little calculation, then changing that expression is easy. If the same one or two or three lines is duplicated throughout the object, not only have you lost the opportunity to communicate its purpose through a well-chosen method name, it is difficult to change.

Debug Print Method

There are many potential reasons to render an object as a string. You might want to present the object to a user, store the object for later retrieval, or present the internals of the object to a programmer.

The Object interface is fairly narrow, containing eleven methods. One of these methods, toString(), renders the receiver as a string, but to what purpose? One temptation is to satisfy several purposes at once. However, these compromises seldom work out. What a bond trader, a programmer, and a database want to know about an object are different.

There is leverage in investing in high-quality debug printing. To discover an important internal detail about an object can require half a minute of mouse clicks. Render that same detail in toString() and the same information is available in a second with a single click. I would rather be figuring out my program during debugging than navigating objects in the development environment. In intense debugging sessions, maintaining focus can save minutes or hours of effort.

Since toString() is public, it is subject to abuse. If an object doesn't support the needed protocol, people have been known to parse the print string to retrieve useful information. Such code is fragile because changing toString() is common. The best policy to prevent such abuse is to do your best to make sure your objects have all the protocol clients need.

Therefore, override toString() when you need to provide a programmer-friendly rendering of an object. Write other string renderings as other methods on the object or in separate classes.

Conversion

Sometimes you have object A and you need object B to pass to some further calculation. How do you represent this conversion from a source object to a destination object?

As with all these patterns, the goal of the conversion patterns is to communicate the programmer's intention clearly. However, there are some technical factors that influence which is the most effective way to express conversion. One of these is the number of conversions needed. If an object only needs to be converted to one other object, you can afford a simple approach. A potentially unbounded number of conversions requires a different approach. Another issue to consider is the dependencies between classes. It's not worth introducing a new dependency just to have a convenient expression of conversion.

The implementation of conversion is a whole separate issue. Sometimes you create a real object of the new type, copying information from the source object. Sometimes you can implement the interface of the destination object without copying information out of the source. As an alternative to conversion, sometimes you can just find a common interface for both objects and code to that.

Conversion Method

If you need to express conversion between objects of similar type, and there are a limited number of conversions, represent conversion as a method on the source object.

For example, suppose you want to implement cartesian and polar coordinates. To create a conversion method, you would implement:

```
class Polar {
  Cartesian asCartesian() {
    ...
  }
}
```

and vice versa. Notice that the return type of the conversion method is a class specific to the destination object. The point of conversion is to get an object with different protocol. Alternatively, you could implement getX() and getY() on

Polar, declare Polar and Cartesian as implementors of Point, and ignore conversion altogether.

Conversion methods have the advantage that they read nicely. They are quite popular (more than one hundred examples in Eclipse, for instance). However, to create one you need to be able to modify the source object's protocol to introduce one. They also introduce a dependency from the source object to the destination object. If such a dependency doesn't already exist, it's not worth introducing one just for the convenience of a conversion method. Finally, conversion methods become unwieldy when there are an unbounded number of potential conversions. A class with twenty different asThis()'s and asThat()'s is hard to read. Alternatively, you might change the clients so they can handle the source object instead of requiring conversion.

These disadvantages lead me to use conversion methods sparingly and only in situations where I am converting to objects of similar type. Otherwise, I use conversion constructors to express conversion.

Conversion Constructor

A conversion constructor takes the source object as a parameter and returns a destination object. A conversion constructor is useful when converting one source object into many destinations because the conversions don't all pile up in the source object.

For example, File supports a conversion constructor that converts a String representing the name of a file into an object suitable for reading, writing, and deleting. While it would be convenient to have String.asFile(), there is no end to the number of such conversions so it's better to have File(String name) and URL(String spec) and StringReadStream(String contents). Otherwise, String would have an unbounded number of conversion methods.

If you need the freedom to implement conversion by returning something other than a concrete class, the conversion constructor can be expressed as a factory method returning a more general type (or placed on a different class than the one created by the method).

Creation

In the olden days (half a century ago), programs were big, undifferentiated masses of code and data. Control could flow from anywhere to anywhere. Data could be accessed from anywhere. Calculations, the original purpose of computers, occurred with (relatively speaking) lightning speed and perfect accuracy. Then people discovered an awkward fact: programs are written as much to be changed as to be run. All this control jumping around and self-modifying code and data accessed from everywhere was great for execution, but it was terrible if you wanted to change the program later. And so began the long and halting road to find models of computation so a change *here* doesn't cause an unanticipated problem *there*.

Smaller programs are generally easier to modify than larger programs. One early strategy to make programs easier to change was to divide the big computer running a big program up into a bunch of smaller computers (objects) running little programs. Objects serve future change by providing an event horizon beyond which changes to the program have low cost.

This subdivision is for human purposes; to accommodate our fallible, changing, inventive minds, not for the good of the computer. The computer runs the same whether the code is one big ugly lump or a lovingly crafted network of mutually supportive objects. For human readers, creating an object makes a statement: some state goes together to support some computation, the details of which are irrelevant for now.

Using object creation expressively requires a balance between the need for clear and direct expression and the need for flexibility. The implementation patterns around creation provide techniques to express variations on the theme of "make me an object".

Complete Constructor

Objects need certain information before they can compute. Communicate the prerequisites to potential users by providing constructors that return objects ready to compute. If there are multiple ways to set up an object, provide multiple constructors, each of which returns a well-formed object.

```
new Rectangle(0, 0, 50, 200);
```

Flexibility is sometimes better served by creating an object with a zero-argument constructor followed by a series of setting methods. However, this approach doesn't communicate what combinations of parameters are required for the correct operation of the object.

```
Rectangle box= new Rectangle();
box.setLeft(0);
box.setWidth(50);
box.setHeight(200);
box.setTop(0);
```

Can I get by without some of these parameters? There is no way to tell by reading the interface. If I see a four-argument constructor, though, I know all four arguments are required.

Constructors commit clients to a concrete class. At the time you write the code invoking the constructor, you may be satisfied that you want to use the concrete class. If you want to make your code more abstract, introduce a factory method. Even if you have a factory method, provide a complete constructor beneath it so curious readers can quickly understand what parameters are needed to create an object.

When implementing a complete constructor, funnel all the constructors to a single master constructor that does all the initialization. This ensures that all the variant constructors will create objects that satisfy all invariants required for proper operation and communicates those invariants to future modifiers of the class.

Factory Method

An alternative way to represent object creation is as a static method on the class. These methods have a couple of advantages over constructors: they can return a more abstract type (a subclass or an implementation of an interface) and they can be named after their intention, not just the class. However, factory methods add complexity, so they should be used when their advantages are valuable, not just as a matter of course.

Cast as a factory method, the Rectangle example would look like this:

```
Rectangle.create(0, 0, 50, 200);
```

If you intend something more complex than creating an object, like recording objects in a cache or creating a subclass that will be decided at runtime, then the factory method is helpful. However, as a reader I am always curious when I see a factory method. What else is going on there beyond object creation? I don't want to waste my readers' time, so if all that's happening is vanilla object creation, I express it as a constructor. If something else is happening at the same time, I introduce a factory method to tip curious readers to this fact.

A variant of a factory method is to gather related factory methods together as instance methods of a special factory object. This is useful when you have several concrete classes that vary at the same time. For example, each operating system could have a different factory object for creating the objects that make operating system calls.

Internal Factory

What do you do when the creation of a helper object is private but complex or subject to change by subclasses? Make a method which creates and returns the new object.

Internal factories are common in lazy initialization. The point of the getter method is stating that the variable is being initialized lazily:

```
getX() {
  if (x == null)
    x= ...;
  return x;
}
```

This is plenty for one method to communicate. If the calculation of x is at all complicated, it can profitably be deferred to an internal factory:

```
getX() {
  if (x == null)
    x= computeX();
  return x;
}
```

Internal factories are also an invitation to refinement by subclasses. A computation that uses the same algorithms on different data structures can be expressed through internal factories. Alternatively, you could pass the data structures as parameters to a helper object.

Collection Accessor Method

Suppose you have an object that contains a collection. How do you provide access to that collection? The simplest solution is providing a getting method for the collection:

```
List<Book> getBooks() {
  return books;
}
```

This gives clients maximum flexibility but creates a variety of problems. Internal state that depends on the contents of the collection can be invalidated behind your back if you return the whole collection. Providing such all-purpose access also passes up an opportunity to create a rich, meaningful protocol for your objects.

One alternative is to wrap the collection in an unmodifiable collection before returning it. Unfortunately, the wrapper only pretends to be a collection for the compiler. An exception is thrown if anyone tries to modify the wrapped collection. Debugging such an error, especially in code in production, is expensive.

```
List<Book> getBooks() {
  return Collections.unmodifiableList(books);
}
```

Instead, offer methods that provide limited, meaningful access to the information in the collection.

```
void addBook(Book arrival) {
  books.add(arrival);
}
int bookCount() {
  return books.size();
}
```

If clients need to iterate over the elements of the collection, provide a method that returns an iterator:

```
Iterator getBooks() {
  return books.iterator();
}
```

This prevents clients from modifying the collection, except for that pesky remove() operation on Iterator. If you want to ensure that clients don't change the contents of the collection, return an iterator that throws an exception if an element is removed. Again, only being notified of the error at runtime is risky and potentially expensive to debug.

```
Iterator<Book> getBooks() {
  final Iterator<Book> reader= books.iterator();
  return new Iterator<Book>() {

    public boolean hasNext() {
      return reader.hasNext();
    }

    public Book next() {
      return reader.next();
    }

    public void remove() {
      throw new UnsupportedOperationException();
    }

  };
}
```

If you find yourself duplicating most of the collection protocols, it's likely you have a design problem. If your object did more work for its clients, it wouldn't have to offer so much access to its innards.

Boolean Setting Method

How best to offer protocol that sets boolean state? The simplest solution is a bare setting method:

```
void setValid(boolean newState) {
  ...
}
```

If clients need the flexibility of this access, this style is fine. However, when all the calls to the setting method are the constants true or false, you can offer a more expressive interface by providing two methods, one for each boolean value:

```
void valid() {...
void invalid() {...
```

Code using this interface reads better, and in such code it is easier to statically discover where state is being set. However, if you see code like this:

```
...
if (...boolean expression...)
  cache.valid();
else
  cache.invalid();
```

go ahead and provide setValidity(boolean) instead.

Query Method

Sometimes an object needs to make a decision based on the state of another object. This isn't ideal, as the other object should generally make decisions for itself. However, when an object needs to offer decision criteria as part of its protocol, do so with a method whose name is prefixed with a form of "be" (like "is" or "was") or "have".

If one object has lots of logic that depends on the state of another object, it's a clue that the logic is misplaced. For example, if a method reads like this:

```
if (widget.isVisible())
  widget.doSomething();
else
  widget.doSomethingElse();
```

then the widget is likely missing a method.

Try moving the logic and seeing if it reads more clearly. Sometimes these moves violate your preconceptions about which object is responsible for what part of a computation. Believing and acting on the evidence of your eyes generally improves the design. The result reads better and is more generally useful than a rigidly maintained picture drawn in advance of experience.

Equality Method

When two objects need to be compared for equality, for example because they are used as keys in a hash table, but their identity doesn't matter, implement equals() and hashCode(). Because two objects that are equal must have the same hash value, compute the hash only using data that is used in computing equality.

For example, if you are writing financial software you might have financial instruments with serial numbers. This could lead you to an equality method like this:

```
Instrument
public boolean equals(Object other) {
  if (! other instanceof Instrument)
    return false;
  Instrument instrument= (Instrument) other;
  return getSerialNumber().equals(instrument.getSerialNumber());
}
```

Note the guard clause at the beginning of the method. In theory, any two objects can be compared for equality, so your code should be prepared for this eventuality. If you know that cross-class comparisons are an indication of a programming error, eliminate the guard clause and allow a ClassCastException to be raised. Either that or throw an IllegalArgumentException inside the guard clause.

Since the serial number is the only information used in comparing equality, it is the only data that should be used in computing the hash value:

```
Instrument
public int hashCode() {
  return getSerialNumber.hashCode();
}
```

Note that for small data sets, 0 works just fine as a hash code.

The whole question of equality seemed more important twenty years ago. I can remember spending considerable time designing elaborate equality schemes. A cartoon that circulated at that time showed two diners sitting at a lunch counter. The first one says to the server, "I'll have what he's having," whereupon the server grabs the second diner's plate and plunks it down in front of the first diner.

Today's equals() and hashCode() are the vestigial remains of that concern with equality. If you are going to use them you need to follow the rules. Don't, and you'll end up with strange defects like putting an object into a collection and not being able to retrieve it immediately afterwards.

Another alternative to fussing with equality is to ensure that if two immutable objects are equal they are the same object. For example, allocating Instruments in a factory method enables this:

```
Instrument
static Instrument create(String serialNumber) {
  if (cache.containsKey(serialNumber))
    return cache.get(serialNumber);
  Instrument result= new Instrument(serialNumber);
  cache.put(serialNumber, result);
  return result;
}
```

Getting Method

One way of providing access to an object's state is to provide a method that returns that state. By convention, in Java these methods are prefixed with "get". For example,

```
int getX() {
  return x;
}
```

This convention is a form of metadata. I briefly tried naming getting methods simply after the variable they returned, but soon reverted. If readers found "getX" easier to read than "x", whatever my personal opinion, it was better to write what was expected.

How to write getting methods is not nearly as important or interesting a question as whether to write them, or at least make them visible. Following the principle of putting logic and data together, the need for public- or package-visible getting methods is a clue that logic should be elsewhere. Rather than writing the getting method, try moving the logic that uses the data instead.

There are a couple of exceptions to my aversion to visible getting methods. One is when I have a set of algorithms located in their own objects. Algorithms need access to data and need a getting method to receive it. Another is when I want a public method and it just so happens to be implemented by returning the value of a field. Finally, getting methods that will be invoked by tools will often have to be public.

Internal getting methods (private or protected) are useful for implementing lazy initialization or caching. As with all additional abstractions, these refinements are best deferred until needed.

Setting Method

If you need a method to set the value of a field, name it after the field prefixed with "set". For example:

```
void setX(int newX) {
  x= newX;
}
```

I'm even more reluctant to make setting methods visible than getting methods. Setting methods are named for implementation, not intention. If a useful bit of an interface is best implemented by setting a field, that's fine, but the name of the method should be written from the client code's perspective. It's better to understand what problem a client is solving by setting a value and provide a method that addresses that problem directly.

Using a setting method as part of the interface lets the implementation leak out:

```
paragraph.setJustification(Paragraph.CENTERED);
```

Naming the interface after the purpose of the method helps the code speak:

```
paragraph.centered();
```

even if the implementation of centered() is a setting method:

```
Paragraph:centered() {
  setJustification(CENTERED);
}
```

Setting methods used internally (private or protected) can be valuable, for instance, for updating dependent information. Our paragraph, for example, might need to redisplay whenever the justification changes. This could be implemented in the setting method:

```
private void setJustification(...) {
  ...
  redisplay();
}
```

This use of a setting method acts like a simple constraint engine, ensuring that if *this* data changes, *that* dependent data over there changes to match (in this case the internals of the paragraph and the information displayed on the screen).

Setting methods make code brittle. One principle is to avoid action at a distance. If object A relies on the details of object B's internal representation, a change to B's code will also require a change to A's code, not because A has changed in any fundamental way, but just because the assumptions on which A is written have changed. Better to move the logic and the data together. Perhaps A should own the data or B should offer more meaningful protocol.

As with getting methods, if you have a tool that needs to invoke setting methods, mark them "Tool Use Only" and make them public. Provide a more communicative and modular interface for humans.

Safe Copy

When using either a getting or setting method, you have potential aliasing problems, where two objects each assume they have exclusive access to a third. Aliasing problems are a symptom of deeper design problems, such as a lack of clarity about which object is responsible for which data, but you can avoid some defects by making a copy of an object before returning it or storing it:

```
List<Book> getBooks() {
  List<Book> result= new ArrayList<Book>();
  result.addAll(books);
  return result;
}
```

In this case it is probably better to provide collection accessor methods instead. However, if you have to provide access to the whole collection, this is a safe way to do it.

Setting methods can also be written with safe copies:

```
void setBooks(List<Book> newBooks) {
  books= new ArrayList<Book>();
  books.addAll(newBooks);
}
```

I remember reviewing one banking system where safe copies were overused. Each accessor method (getter or setter) had two versions, one "safe" and the other not. To eliminate aliasing defects, huge object structures were copied every time a safe copying method was invoked. The system was too slow, so clients tended to use the unsafe version, which resulted in a host of aliasing defects. The underlying design problem, that objects weren't offering enough meaningful protocol, was never addressed.

Safe copying is strictly a palliative, to be used to protect code from uncontrolled outside access. It should rarely be part of the core semantics of an implementation. Immutable objects and composed methods provide simpler, more communicative interfaces that are less prone to error.

Conclusion

This chapter has described the patterns for creating methods. This concludes the patterns related to the Java language. The following chapter describes patterns for using the collection classes.

Chapter 9

Collections

I must say that I didn't expect this chapter to amount to much. When I started writing it, I thought I would end up with an API document—types and operations. The basic idea is simple: a collection distinguishes between objects in the collection and those not in the collection. What more was there to say?

What I discovered is that collections are a far richer topic than I ever suspected, both in their structure and the possibilities they offer for communicating intent. The concept of collections blends several different metaphors. The metaphor you emphasize changes how you use collections. Each of the collection interfaces communicates a different variation on the theme of a sack of objects. Each of the implementations also communicates variations, mostly with regard to performance. The result is that mastering collections is a big part of learning to communicate well with code.

Collection-like behavior used to be implemented by providing links in the data structure itself: each page in a document would have links to the previous and next pages. More recently, the fashion has swung to using a separate object for the collection which relates elements. This allows the flexibility to put the same object in several different collections without modifying the object.

Collections are important because they are a way of expressing one of the most fundamental kinds of variation in programming, the variation of number. Variation in logic is expressed with conditionals or polymorphic messages. Variation in the cardinality of data is expressed by putting the data into a collection. The precise details of that collection reveal much about the intention of the original programmer to a reader.

There is an old (by computer terms) saying that the only interesting numbers are 0, 1 and many (this saying was not written by a numerical analyst). If the absence of a field expresses "zero" and the presence of a field expresses "one", then a field holding a collection is a way of expressing "many".

Collections hover in a strange world halfway between a programming language construct and a library. Collections are so universally useful, and their use is so well understood, that it almost seems time to have a mainstream language that allows statements like `plural unique Book books;` instead of the current `Collection<Book> books= new HashSet<Book>();`. Until collections are first-class language elements, it is important to know how to use the current collection library to express common ideas in straightforward ways.

The remainder of the chapter is divided into six parts: the metaphors behind collections, the issues to be expressed through the use of collections, the collection interfaces and what they mean to the reader, the collection implementations and what they say, an overview of functions available in the `Collections` class, and finally a discussion of extending collections through inheritance.

Metaphors

As suggested above, collections blend different metaphors. The first is that of a multi-valued variable. There is a sense in which a variable that refers to a collection is really a variable referring to several objects at the same time. Looked at this way, the collection disappears as a separate object. The collection's identity is not interesting, only the objects to which it refers. As with all variables, you can assign to a multi-valued variable (add and remove elements), retrieve its value, and send the variable messages (with the `for` loop).

The multi-valued variable metaphor breaks down in Java because collections are separate objects with identity. The second metaphor mixed into collections is that of objects—a collection is an object. You can retrieve a collection, pass it around, test it for equality, and send it messages. Collections can be shared between objects, although this creates the possibility of aliasing problems. Because collections are a set of related interfaces and implementations, they are open to extension, both with expanded interfaces and new implementations. So, just as collections "are" multi-valued variables, they also "are" objects.

The combination of the two metaphors makes for some strange effects. Because a collection is implemented as an object that can be passed around, you get the equivalent of call-by-reference, where instead of passing a variable's contents to a routine, you pass the variable itself. Changes to the variable's value are reflected in the calling routine. Call-by-reference went out of fashion in language design a couple of decades ago because of the possibility for unintended consequences. It was hard to debug programs when you couldn't be certain of all the places where a variable could be modified. Some of the conventions for programming with collections exist to avoid situations where it is hard to read the code and predict where a collection could be modified.

A third metaphor useful for thinking about collections is that of mathematical sets. A collection is a sack of objects just like a mathematical set is a sack of elements. A set divides the world into things in the set and things not in the set. A collection divides the world of objects into objects that are in the collection and objects that are not. Two basic operations on mathematical sets are finding their cardinality (the size() method of collections) and testing for inclusion (represented by the contains() method).

The mathematical metaphor is only approximate for collections. The other basic operations on sets—union, intersection, difference, and symmetric difference—are not directly represented by collections. Whether this is because these operations are intrinsically less useful or because they aren't used because they aren't available makes for an interesting debate.

Issues

Collections are used to express several orthogonal concepts in programs. In principle, you should express yourself as precisely as possible. With collections, this means using the most general possible interface as a declaration and the most specific implementation class. However, this is not an absolute rule. I carefully went through JUnit and generalized all the variable declarations. The result was a mess, because there was no uniformity. The confusion of having the same object declared as an Iterable in one spot, a Collection in another, and a List elsewhere made reading the code more difficult without much payoff. It was clearer to just declare every variable as a List.

The first concept expressed by collections is their size. Arrays (which are primitive collections) have a fixed size, set when the array is created. Most collections can change size after they are created.

A second concept expressed through collections is whether or not the order of elements is important. Calculations in which the elements affect each other or where external users of the calculation attach importance to order call for collections that preserve order. The order may be the order in which elements were added or it may be provided by some outside influence like lexicographic comparison.

Another issue to be expressed by collections is the uniqueness of elements. There are computations where the presence or absence of an element is sufficient, others where an element needs to be able to be present multiple times in a collection for the computation to be correct.

How are the elements accessed? Sometimes it is enough to iterate over the elements, doing some calculation with them one at a time. At other times it is important to be able to store and retrieve elements with a key.

Finally, performance considerations are communicated through choice of collection. If a linear search is fast enough, a generic Collection is good enough. If the collection grows too large it will be important to be able to test for or access elements by a key, suggesting a Set or Map. Time and space can both be optimized through the judicious selection of collections.

Sidebar: Performance

Most programmers don't have to worry about the performance of small-scale operations most of the time. This is a refreshing change from the old days, when performance tuning was daily business. However, computing resources are not infinite. When experience has shown that performance needs to be better and measurement has shown where the bottlenecks are, it is important to express performance-related decisions clearly. Many times, better performance results in less of some other quality in the code, like readability or flexibility. It is important to pay as little as possible for the needed performance.

Coding for performance can violate the principle of local consequences. A small change to one part of a program can degrade performance in another part. If a method works efficiently only if the collection it is passed can test for membership quickly, then an innocent substitution of ArrayList for HashSet elsewhere in the program can make the method intolerably slow. Distant consequences are another argument for coding carefully when coding for performance.

Performance is connected with collections because most collections can grow without limit. The data structure holding the characters I am typing right now needs to be able to hold millions of characters. I would like inserting the millionth character to be just as fast as inserting the first.

My overall strategy for performance coding with collections is to use the simplest possible implementation at first and pick a more specialized collection class when it becomes necessary. When I make performance-related decisions I try to localize them as much as possible even if that requires some changes to the design. Then, when the performance is good enough again, I stop tuning.

Interfaces

Readers of collection-based code are looking for answers to different questions when they look at the interfaces you have declared for your variables and the implementations you chose for those variables. The interface declaration tells the reader about the collection: whether the collection is in a particular order, whether there are duplicate elements, and whether there is any way to look up elements by key or only through iteration.

The interfaces described below are:

- Array—Arrays are the simplest and least flexible collection: fixed size, simple accessing syntax, and fast.

- Iterable—The basic collection interface, allowing a collection to be used for iteration but nothing else.

- Collection—Offers adding, removing, and testing for elements.

- List—A collection whose elements are ordered and can be accessed by their location in the collection (i.e., "give me the third element").

- Set—A collection with no duplicates.

- SortedSet—An ordered collection with no duplicates.

- Map—A collection whose elements are stored and retrieved by key.

Array

Arrays are the simplest interface for collections. Unfortunately, they don't have the same protocol as other collections, so it's harder to change from an array to a collection than from one kind of collection to another. Unlike most collections, the size of an array is fixed when it is created. Arrays are also different as they are built into the language, not provided by a library.

Arrays are more efficient in time and space than other collections for simple operations. The timing tests I did to accompany writing this suggest that array access (i.e. elements[i]) is more than ten times faster than the equivalent ArrayList operation (elements.get(i)). (As these numbers vary substantially in different operating environments, if you care about the performance difference you should time the operations yourself.) The flexibility of the other collection classes makes them more valuable in most cases, but arrays are a handy trick to be able to pull out when you need more performance in a small part of an application.

Iterable

Declaring a variable Iterable only says that it contains multiple values. Iterable is the basis for the loop construct in Java 5. Any object declared as Iterable can be used in a for loop. This is implemented by quietly calling the method iterator().

One of the issues to be communicated when using collections is whether clients are expected to modify them. Unfortunately, Iterable and its helper, Iterator, provide no way to state declaratively that a collection shouldn't be modified. Once you have an Iterator, you can invoke its remove() method, which deletes an element from the underlying Iterable. While your Iterables are safe from having elements added, they can have elements removed without the object that owns the collection being notified.

As described in "Collection Accessor Method" on page 91, there are a few ways to ensure that a collection is not modified: wrapping it in a unmodifiable collection, creating a custom iterator that throws an exception when a client tries to modify the collection, or returning a safe copy.

Iterable is simple. It doesn't even allow you to measure the size of instances; all you can do is iterate over the elements. Sub-interfaces of Iterable provide more useful behavior.

Collection

Collection inherits from Iterable, but it adds methods to add, remove, search for and count elements. Declaring a variable or method as a Collection leaves many options for an implementation class. By leaving the declaration as vaguely specified as possible, you retain the freedom to change implementation classes later without having the change ripple through the code.

Collections are a bit like the mathematical notion of sets, except that the operations performing the equivalent of union, intersection, and difference (addAll(), retainAll(), and removeAll()) modify the receiver instead of returning newly allocated collections.

List

To Collection, List adds the idea that elements are in a stable order. An element can be retrieved by providing its index to the collection. A stable sequence is important when the elements of a collection interact with each other. For example, a queue of messages that should be processed in their arrival order should be stored in a list.

Set

A Set is a collection that contains no duplicates (elements that would report that they are equal() to each other). This corresponds closely to the mathematical notion of set, although the metaphor is thin because adding an element to a Set modifies the collection rather than returning a new collection including the added element.

A Set discards information that most collections keep—the number of times an element appears. This is not a problem in cases where the presence or absence of an element is interesting but the number of times the element appears is not. For example, if I want to know who all the authors of books are in a library, I don't care how many books each author wrote. I just want to know who they are. A Set is an appropriate way to implement such a query.

The elements in a Set are in no particular order. Just because you iterate through them in a certain order once does not mean that the elements will appear in the same order the next time. This lack of predictable order is not a limitation in cases where the elements don't interact with each other.

Sometimes you want to store duplicates in a collection but remove them for a particular operation. Create a temporary Set and pass it to the operation:

```
printAuthors(new HashSet<Author>(getAuthors()));
```

SortedSet

The ordering and uniqueness attributes of collections are not mutually exclusive. At times you'd like to keep a collection in order but eliminate duplicates. SortedSet stores ordered-but-unique elements.

Unlike the ordering of a List, which is related to the order in which elements were added or by explicit indexes passed to add(int, Object), the ordering in a SortedSet is provided by a Comparator. In the absence of an explicit order, the "natural order" of the elements is used. For example, strings are sorted in lexicographical order.

To compute the authors contributing to a library, you could use a SortedSet:

```
public Collection<String> getAlphabeticalAuthors() {
  SortedSet<String> results= new TreeSet<String>();
  for (Book each: getBooks())
    results.add(each.getAuthor());
  return results;
}
```

This example uses the default sorting of strings. If a Book had its author represented by an object, the code above might look like this:

```
public Collection<String> getAlphabeticalAuthors() {
  Comparator<Author> sorter= new Comparator<Author>() {
    public int compare(Author o1, Author o2) {
      if (o1.getLastName().equals(o2.getLastName()))
        return o1.getFirstName().compareTo(o2.getFirstName());
      return o1.getLastName().compareTo(o2.getLastName());
    }
  };
  SortedSet<String> results= new TreeSet<String>(sorter);
  for (Book each: getBooks())
    results.add(each.getAuthor());
  return results;
}
```

Map

The final collection interface is Map, which is a hybrid of the other interfaces. A Map stores values by key, but unlike a List, the key can be any object and not just an integer. The keys of a Map must be unique, a bit like sets, although the values can contain duplicates. The elements of a Map are in no particular order, also like a Set.

Because Map is not completely like any of the other collection interfaces, it stands alone, not inheriting from any of them. Maps are two collections at the same time; a collection of keys connected to a collection of values. You can't simply ask a Map for its iterator, because it is not clear whether you want an iterator over the keys, over the values, or over the pairs of keys-and-values.

Maps are useful for implementing two of the implementation patterns: extrinsic state and variable state. Extrinsic state suggests storing special-purpose data related to an object separately from the object itself. One way to implement extrinsic state is with a Map whose keys are the objects and whose values are the related data. In variable state, different instances of the same class store different data fields. To implement this, have the object hold a map which maps from strings (representing the names of the virtual fields) to the values.

Implementations

Choosing implementation classes for collections is primarily a matter of performance. As with all performance issues, it is best to pick a simple implementation to begin with and then tune based on experience.

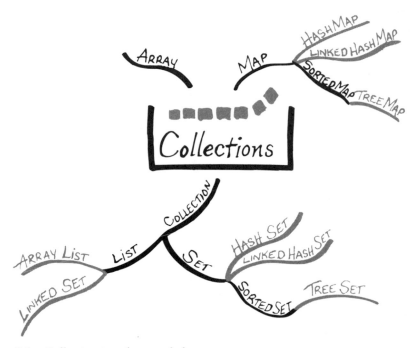

Figure 9.1 *Collection interfaces and classes*

In this section, each interface introduces alternative implementations. Because performance considerations dominate the choice of implementation class, each set of alternatives is accompanied by performance measurements for important operations. Appendix, "Performance Measurement," provides the source code for the tool I used to gather this data.

By far the majority of collections are implemented by ArrayList, with HashSet a distant second (~3400 references to ArrayList in Eclipse+JDK versus ~800 references to HashSet). The quick-and-dirty solution is to choose whichever of these classes suits your needs. However, for those times when experience shows that performance matters, the remainder of this section presents the details of the alternative implementations.

A final factor in choosing a collection implementation class is the size of the collections involved. The data presented below shows the performance of collections sized one to one hundred thousand. If your collections only contain one or two elements, your choice of implementation class may be different than if you expect them to scale to millions of elements. In any case, the gains available from switching implementation classes are often limited, and you'll need to look for larger-scale algorithmic changes if you want to further improve performance.

Collection

The default class to use when implementing a Collection is ArrayList. The potential performance problem with ArrayList is that contains(Object) and other operations that rely on it like remove(Object) take time proportional to the size of the collection. If a performance profile shows one of these methods to be a bottleneck, consider replacing your ArrayList with a HashSet. Before doing so, make sure that your algorithm is insensitive to discarding duplicate elements. When you have data that is already guaranteed to contain no duplicates, the switch won't make a difference. Figure 9.2 compares the performance of ArrayList and HashSet. (See Appendix A for the details of how I collected this information.)

List

To the Collection protocol, List adds the idea that the elements are in a stable order. The two implementations of List in common use are ArrayList and LinkedList.

The performance profiles of these two implementations are mirror images. ArrayList is fast at accessing elements and slow at adding and removing elements, while LinkedList is slow at accessing elements and fast at adding and removing elements (see Figure 9.3). If you see a profile dominated by calls to add() or remove(), consider switching an ArrayList to a LinkedList.

Set

There are three main implementations of Set: HashSet, LinkedHashSet, and TreeSet (which actually implements SortedSet). HashSet is the fastest but its elements are in no guaranteed order. A LinkedHashSet maintains elements in the order in which they were added, but at the cost of an extra 30% time penalty for adding and removing elements (see Figure 9.3). TreeSet keeps its elements sorted according to a Comparator but at the cost of making adding and removing elements or testing for an element take time proportional to $\log n$, where n is the size of the collection.

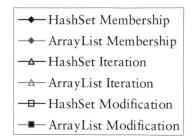

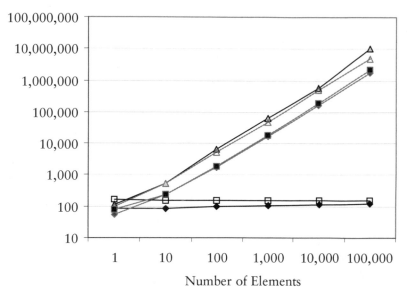

Figure 9.2 *Comparing ArrayList and HashSet as implementations of Collection*

Choose a LinkedHashSet if you need the order of elements to be stable. External users, for example, may appreciate getting elements in the same order each time.

Map

The implementations of Map follow a similar pattern to the implementations of Set. HashMap is the fastest and simplest. LinkedHashMap preserves the order of elements, iterating over the elements in the order in which they were inserted. TreeMap (actually an implementation of SortedMap) iterates over entries based on the order of the keys, but at the cost of making insertion and inclusion testing take time propor-

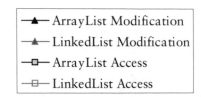

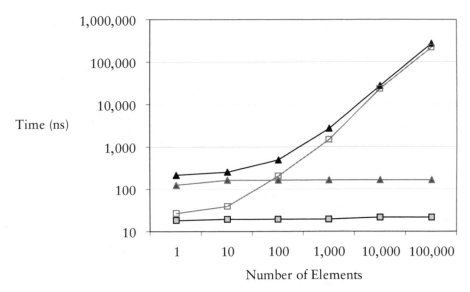

Figure 9.3 *Comparing ArrayList and LinkedList*

tional to *log n*. Figure 9.5 summarizes the way performance scales for these Map implementations.

Collections

The utility class Collections is a library class that provides collection functionality that doesn't fit neatly into any of the collection interfaces. Here is a quick overview of what is available.

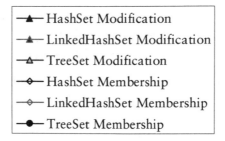

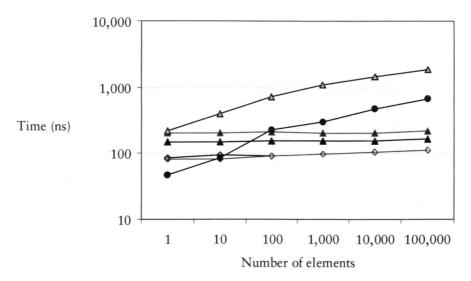

Figure 9.4 *Comparing Set implementations.*

Searching

The indexOf() operation takes time proportional to the size of the list. However, if the elements are sorted, binary search can find the index of an element in $log_2\ n$ time. Call Collections.binarySearch(list, element) to return the index of an element in the list. If the element does not appear in the list, a negative number will be returned. If the list is not sorted, the results are unpredictable.

Binary search only improves performance for lists with constant-time random access, like ArrayList (see Figure 9.6).

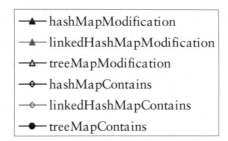

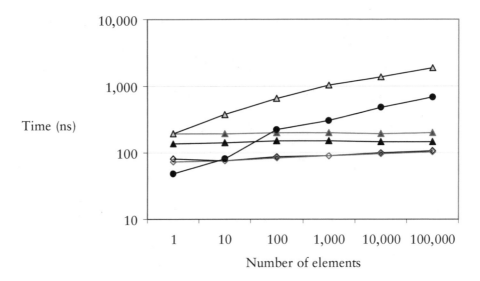

Figure 9.5   *Comparing Map implementations*

Sorting

Collections also provides operations to change the order of the elements of a list. Reverse(list) reverses the order of all the elements of the list. Shuffle(list) places the elements in random order. Sort(list) and sort(list, comparator) place the elements in ascending order. Unlike binary search, sorting performance is roughly the same for ArrayList and LinkedList, because the elements are first copied into an array, the array is sorted, and then the elements are copied back (run the timer test Sorting in Appendix A to verify this).

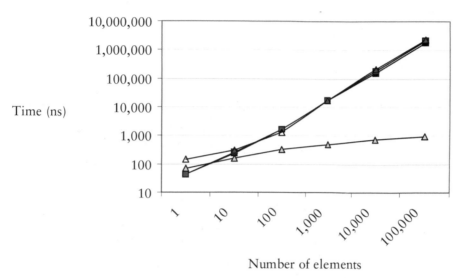

Figure 9.6 *Comparing indexOf() and binary search*

Unmodifiable Collections

As mentioned in the discussion of Iterable above, even the most basic collection interfaces allow collections to be modified. If you are passing a collection to untrusted code, you can ensure that it won't be modified by having Collections wrap it in an implementation that throws a runtime exception if clients try to modify it. There are variants that work with Collection, List, Set, and Map.

```
@Test(expected=UnsupportedOperationException.class)
public void unmodifiableCollectionsThrowExceptions() {
  List<String> l= new ArrayList<String>();
  l.add("a");
  Collection<String> unmodifiable= Collections.unmodifiableCollection(l);
  Iterator<String> all= unmodifiable.iterator();
  all.next();
  all.remove();
}
```

Single-Element Collections

If you have a single element and you need to pass it to an interface that expects a collection, you can quickly convert it by calling Collections.singleton(), which returns a Set. There are also variants that convert to a List or Map. All the collections returned are not modifiable.

```
@Test public void exampleOfSingletonCollections() {
  Set<String> longWay= new HashSet<String>();
  longWay.add("a");
  Set<String> shortWay= Collections.singleton("a");
  assertEquals(shortWay, longWay);
}
```

Empty Collections

Similarly, if you need to use an interface that expects a collection and you know you have no elements, Collections will create an unmodifiable empty collection for you.

```
@Test public void exampleOfEmptyCollection() {
  assertTrue(Collections.emptyList().isEmpty());
}
```

Extending Collections

I have often seen classes that extend one of the collection classes. A Library holding a list of books, for example, could be implemented by extending ArrayList:

```
class Library extends ArrayList {...}
```

This declaration provides implementations of add() and remove(), iteration, and the other collection operations.

There are several problems with extending collection classes to get collection-ish behavior. First, many of the operations offered by collections will be inappropriate for clients. For example, clients generally shouldn't be able to clear() a Library or convert it toArray(). At the very least, the metaphors are mixed and confusing. At worst, all these operations need to be disinherited by implementing them and throwing an UnsupportedOperationException. It's not a good trade-off to inherit a few useful lines of code but spend far more lines eliminating functionality you don't want. The second problem with inheriting from collection classes is that it wastes inheritance, a precious resource. To pick up a few lines of useful implementation, you preclude using inheritance in some more highly leveraged way.

In such a situation, it is better to delegate to a collection rather than inherit from one:

```
class Library {
  Collection<Book> books= new ArrayList<Book>();
  ...
}
```

With this design, you can reveal only those operations that make sense and you can give them meaningful names. You are free to use inheritance to share implementation with other model classes. If a Library offers access to books by several different keys, you can name the operations appropriately:

```
Book getBookByISBN(ISBN);
Book getBookByID(UniqueID);
```

Only extend collections if you are implementing a general-purpose collection class, something that could be added to java.util. In all other cases, store elements in a subsidiary collection.

Conclusion

This chapter has described the patterns for using the collection classes. This concludes the patterns for Java and its collection classes. The preceding patterns were all written with a bias towards application development, where simplicity and ease of communication drive costs down but it is possible to change the design of the whole application at once. The following chapter describes how to modify these patterns when building frameworks, where complexity is acceptable if it preserves the ability to continue evolving the framework without being able to change all application code.

Chapter 10

Evolving Frameworks

The preceding implementation patterns assume that changing code is cheap compared to understanding and communicating the intent of code. This has been true of most of my development experience. However, framework development, in which client code can't be changed by the framework developers, violates this assumption. Changing the design of JUnit, for example, is generally easy to accomplish but can be very expensive to deploy if the host of downstream tool makers and test writers have to change their code as well. Incompatible updates are so expensive that we avoid such updates as much as possible.

When we released JUnit 4 recently we spent nearly half of our engineering budget on reducing the cost of deployment for our clients. We tried to make sure that new-style tests would work with old tools and old-style tests would work with new tools. We also worked to make sure we had the freedom to make future changes to JUnit without breaking client code.

This chapter sketches out how implementation patterns change when developing frameworks. It talks about the challenges of framework development, how to reduce the impact of incompatible upgrades, and how to design frameworks to avoid incompatible upgrades. Evolving frameworks while minimizing the disruption for clients requires additional complexity in the framework, reducing the client-visible features, and careful communication about the changes that are necessary.

Changing Frameworks without Changing Applications

The fundamental dilemma in developing and maintaining frameworks is that they need to evolve but there is a large cost to breaking existing client code. The perfect framework upgrade adds new functionality without changing any existing functionality. Compatible upgrades are not always possible, however.

Maintaining backward compatibility often adds complexity to the framework. At some point, the cost of maintaining perfect compatibility outweighs the value to clients. Improving the economics of framework development relies on reducing the probability of an incompatible upgrade and reducing the cost of such upgrades when they are necessary. While in conventional development reducing complexity to a minimum is a valuable strategy for making the code easy to understand, in framework development it is often more cost-effective to add complexity in order to enhance the framework developer's ability to improve the framework without breaking client code.

While compatibility holds increased importance for framework development, simplicity is still an important value. Complex frameworks are less likely to be used than simple ones. Add the least possible complexity in order to maintain a balance between future freedom for development and cost for clients.

A trend in the preceding implementation patterns was for code to be as broadly applicable as possible while still being easy to understand. In framework development applicability is sacrified to gain future freedom to change the design. For example, I tend to make fields protected in most of my code, but while developing frameworks I make them private. This makes my superclasses harder for clients to use, but allows me to change my framework data representations without affecting clients' applications. A framework with all protected fields would be more immediately usable but harder to evolve later.

The goal is frameworks that are complex enough to evolve but simple enough to be used and narrowly applicable enough to evolve but widely applicable enough to be useful. These additional constraints on design are what make framework development riskier and more expensive than application development. Fortunately, variants of the implementation patterns can help you build, deploy and modify frameworks that are both useful and amenable to change.

Incompatible Upgrades

Even if a framework upgrade could potentially break client code, there are ways to reduce the cost of the upgrade for clients. Staging the upgrade in small steps gives clients warning of what is coming and lets them decide when to make the investment in changing their code. For example, deprecating code but leaving it functioning for one or more releases sends the message that clients need to move to the new API. Deprecation is an example of the more general strategy of maintaining two different architectures for solving the same problem. The parallel architectures add complexity but reduce the disruption of upgrading.

The Java collection classes demonstrate parallel architectures. The old Vector and Enumerator classes were made forward-compatible when the new classes rooted on Collection were introduced. Now (and forever, in the case of Java) you can run code using the older collections.

Packages can provide a way to offer clients incremental access to upgrades. By introducing new classes in a new package, you can give them the same name as the old classes. For example, if I can upgrade org.junit.Assert in org.junit.newandimproved.Assert, then clients need only change the import statements to be using the new class. Changing imports is less risky and intrusive than changing code.

Another incremental strategy is to change either the API or the implementation but not both in the same release. The intermediate release, with either the new interface to the old code or the old interface to the new code, gives everyone, framework providers and clients alike, time to get used to the direction of change. There is time to resolve any technical problems caused by the new approach while the problems are still small.

The collection classes bring up another point about upgrading frameworks: retiring obsolete functionality. Part of the agreement between framework provider and client is how often client code will be forced to upgrade to work with a new framework release. Sun's commitment is that old code will work in perpetuity. Eclipse, by comparison, agrees to maintain compatibility only within integer releases. As a framework provider, you'll need to carefully balance the need to quickly evolve your framework with your clients' need to work with a stable platform as you choose a retirement strategy.

Eclipse provides an example of another way to reduce the cost of incompatible upgrades: offer automated tools to upgrade client code. Eclipse reduced the cost of the potentially incompatible 2.x to 3.0 upgrade by making sure that most 2.x plug-ins would work unchanged in release 3.0, but also offered a conversion tool to make 2.x plug-ins fully 3.0 compliant. The tool added necessary files and moved functionality between files so old code worked natively in the new version. By combining strategies, Eclipse maintains much of their freedom to improve their rapidly evolving framework while still serving their existing clients with mostly stable functionality.

You can reduce the cost of changing code if clients can switch to your upgraded functionality with a simple find/replace operation. If the name of a method changes, it will be cheaper for clients if you leave the arguments in the same order. Perhaps someday it will be possible to pass around sets of refactorings along with framework upgrades, but for now reducing the cost of upgrades may limit your design options.

Another factor in managing incompatible upgrades is the composition and growth of your client community. If your current clients are eager to use the latest functionality, they will be willing to make the effort to upgrade. If an upgrade allows you to dramatically increase your client base then you may be willing to endure some grumbling from existing clients. Today's complaints from 400 customers won't seem so significant if in six months you have 4000 happy customers. Take care not to alienate real customers for phantasms, leaving yourself with an upgraded framework and no clients at all.

This section has detailed how to manage incompatible framework upgrades. By far the more desirable situation is an upgrade that introduces new funtionality without affecting existing client code. The remainder of this chapter discusses the implementation patterns for writing frameworks you can upgrade without disrupting clients.

Encouraging Compatible Change

For a framework upgrade to maintain compatibility, client code should rely on as few details of your framework as possible. However, client code has to rely on some details or there isn't any reason for your framework to exist at all. Ideally, clients will rely only on details that you don't want to change. Since your growth and change are unpredictable, you can't decide up-front which details you won't want to change. You can play the odds, however: reducing the number of visible details and revealing details that are less likely to change, delivering useful functionality while retaining the freedom to change the design.

One decision to make is what variants of compatibility you are going to offer. Is your upgrade backward-compatible, so clients can still invoke old methods and pass old objects to your framework? Is your upgrade forward-compatible, so you can pass new-style objects to clients and they will work like the old objects? The style or styles of compatibility you choose affect how much effort will go into developing and testing an upgrade. Our latest release of JUnit, for example, was much more expensive because we chose to offer both forward and backward compatibility. Users reported several defects with compatibility that we didn't consider while we were coding. I'm satisfied with our compatibility decision. We had a huge base of existing tests to support and clients who for the most part weren't rushing to upgrade. However, supporting both forward and backward compatibility had surprising consequences.

Most frameworks in Java are represented as objects that are created, used, or refined by clients. This section describes how to represent frameworks so clients can use the functionality they need and at the same time the framework developer can continue evolving the framework. Striking this balance requires careful attention to how objects are used, how they are created, and how methods are structured.

Library Class

One simple and fairly future-proof style of API is the library class. If you can represent all of your functionality as procedure calls with simple parameters then clients are well insulated from future changes. When you release a new version of your library class you need only ensure that all existing methods work the same as they did before. New functionality is represented as new procedures or new variants of existing procedures.

The Collections class is an example of an API represented as a library class. Clients use it by invoking static methods, not by instantiating it. New versions of the collection classes add new static methods, leaving the existing functionality unchanged.

The big problem with representing an API as a library class is the limited number of concepts and variants that can be easily expressed. As variations of functionality and cross-products of variations proliferate it is easy for the number of needed procedures to explode. Additionally, clients can only change the data they send to the framework; they can't plug in any variations in logic.

Objects

Assuming that you are going to represent your framework as objects, you have a tougher task balancing simplicity and complexity, flexibility and specificity so the framework is both useful and stable for clients and evolvable for you. The trick is, as much as you can manage it, to write the framework so that clients rely only on details that are unlikely to change.

I'll discuss four issues in representing a framework as objects:

- Style of use—Will clients use the framework by instantiating your objects, configuring your objects, and/or by refining or implementing your objects?

- Abstraction—Will you represent class-level details as interfaces or classes? How will you use visibility to reveal only relatively stable details?

- Creation—How will objects be created?

- Methods—How will your methods be structured so as to be useful to clients and amenable to change?

Style of Use

Frameworks can support three main styles of use: instantiation, configuration, and implementation. Each style offers different combinations of usability, flexibility, and stability. You can also mix these styles in a single framework to provide a better balance of design freedom for framework developers and power for clients.

The simplest style of use is instantiation. When I want a server socket I write `new ServerSocket()`. Once instantiated, a framework object works by invoking methods on it. Instantiation works when the only form of variation clients need is variation in data, not logic.

Configuration is a more complex and flexible style of use in which the client creates framework objects but passes them his own objects to be called at predetermined times. A `TreeSet`, for example, can be called with a client-defined `Comparator` to allow for arbitrary sorting of elements.

```
Comparator<Author> byFirstName= new Comparator<Author>() {
  public int compare(Author book1, Author book2) {
    return book1.getFirstName().compareTo(book2.getFirstName());
  }
};
SortedSet<Author> sorted= new TreeSet<Author>(byFirstName);
```

Configuration is more flexible than instantiation because it can accommodate variations in logic as well as data. However, it offers less freedom to the framework designer because once you begin calling a client object, you need to continue calling that object in the same way and at the same time or risk breaking client code. Another limitation of configuration is that it can only handle a few dimensions of variability. A given object can only have one or two options for configuration before it becomes too complex to use easily.

When clients need more ways to hook in their own logic than those provided by configuration, then you can offer use by implementation. In implementation, clients create their own classes which are used by the framework. As long as the client class extends a framework class or implements a framework interface (how to choose is covered in the following section), the client is free to include whatever logic he likes.

Of the three styles of using objects, implementation has the most potential to restrict future design freedom. Every detail of the framework-supplied superclass or interface needs to be preserved if you want to guarantee that client code will continue to work. Every detail you reveal in a framework abstraction is a two-edged sword—offering the client a place to hook his code, but committing the framework developer to either supporting the detail or risk breaking client code.

The Comparator example above demonstrates a simple version of the implementation style of framework use. The byFirstName comparator is an implementation of the collection framework's comparator abstraction (in this case a class). In this case the implementation is simple because there is only one bit of logic to be plugged in and it is short enough to appear in-line with the rest of the code. Implementations can also reside in inner classes or standalone classes if they are more complex.

The implementation style of use scales much better than configuration because it can handle any number of independent variations, each represented by a hook method defined by the framework.

JUnit mixes all four styles of use:

- JUnitCore is a library class with a static run(Class...) method to run all the tests in all the classes.

- JUnitCore is also instantiable, with instances providing finer control over test running and notification.

- The @Test, @Before, and @After annotations are a form of configuration where test writers can identify bits of code to be run at certain times.

- The @RunWith annotation is a form of implementation, where test writers who need non-standard test-running behavior can implement their own runners.

Abstraction

The implementation style of framework use introduces the question of whether to represent abstract entities as an interface or a common superclass. Each approach has pluses and minuses for framework developers and clients. The two approaches aren't mutually exclusive either. A framework can offer clients both an interface and a default implementation of that interface.

Interface

The big advantage of offering clients an interface is that interfaces record so few details. Clients can't "accidentally" use more of the framework than intended. This protection comes at a cost, however. As long as interfaces remain unchanged they are fine, but introducing a new method to an interface will break all the client implementations of that interface. If you can ensure that clients only use an interface, not implement it, though, then you can introduce new methods without breaking client code. In spite of the brittleness of interfaces, they are widely used in the Java world to express abstractions, which is itself an argument in their favor.

Interfaces have the minor advantage that client classes can implement several of them at a time. Implementing several related interfaces in a single class can be a clear and direct way to communicate. However, a class that simultaneously implements completely unrelated interfaces is probably best broken up in order to communicate its purposes more clearly.

A variation of interfaces that provides some additional flexibility at the cost of some complexity is versioned interfaces. If you add operations to an interface, you break client code. However, you can create a sub-interface and put the new operations there. Clients can pass objects conforming to the new interface wherever the old interface is expected, but existing code continues working as before.

This additional flexibility comes at the cost of greater framework complexity. The framework has to explicitly dispatch at runtime whenever it wants to invoke operations on the new interface. For example, AWT has two versions of the layout manager interface. In half a dozen places, AWT has code like this:

```
...
if (layout instanceof LayoutManager2) {
  LayoutManager2 layout2= (LayoutManager2) layout;
  layout2.newOperation();
}
...
```

Versioned interfaces are a reasonable compromise when you absolutely must introduce new operations to an existing interface-based abstraction without affecting client code. They are not a long-term solution for frequently changing abstraction, because of the complexity they create both for client and framework developers. Changing abstractions should be represented as superclasses to accommodate change gracefully.

Superclass

The alternative to defining an abstraction by an interface is to ask clients to pass an instance of a class or one of its subclasses. The advantages and disadvantages of this style are the inverse of those for interfaces: classes can specify more details than interfaces, but adding an operation to a superclass doesn't break existing code. Unlike interfaces, though, client classes can only extend a single framework class.

The details of a superclass visible to clients are the public and protected methods and fields of the superclass. Each such method or field is a promise not to change. If too many details are visible, that can be an awful lot of promises, severely constraining future design changes.

Care when writing a superclass can reduce these constraints to essentially what is available through interfaces. Fields in a framework should always be private. If clients need access to the data in fields, provide it through getters. Carefully examine your methods and make only essential methods public or, better yet, protected. Following these rules allows you to define a superclass that exposes only a few more details than the equivalent interface but allows clients more flexibility to hook in their own logic.

The abstract keyword gives you a way of communicating to clients where they are required to fill in logic. Providing a reasonable default implementation of methods where possible gives clients the ability to get started easily. However, introducing new abstract methods in a superclass creates an incompatible upgrade because clients must implement the methods before their subclasses will compile again.

The final keyword when applied to a class prevents clients from creating subclasses, enforcing the instantiation or configuration style of framework use. When applied to a method, it allows the framework developer to assume that particular code is being executed, even in a client-visible method. While I respect framework developers' perogative to simplify their programming tasks, I have also been frustrated by final classes and methods. I once spent two days trying fruitlessly to programmatically create SWT events for testing. It was (unnecessarily it seemed to me) final classes that prevented me from coding what I needed. I ended up writing my own event classes that duplicated the SWT events so I could test without a GUI. Saving final for situations where it has substantial payoff for you and poses few problems for clients will improve framework developer/client relations.

While I am on the topic of visibility I should point out that there is a hole in the Java packaging scheme. Frameworks that are organized into several packages need a visibility declaration that states, "Visible within the framework but not to clients." One solution to this problem is to separate packages into published and internal and to communicate the difference by including the name "internal" in the internal package paths. In Eclipse, for example, you will see packages like org.eclipse.jdt... and org.eclipse.jdt.internal....

Internal packages provide middle ground between revealing and concealing framework details. Clients can choose for themselves how much responsibility they want to accept for building on top of potentially unstable parts of the framework. Sometimes the functionality you need as a client is there in the framework, it was just misclassified (from your perspective) by the framework developers.

Creation

If your framework publishes any concrete classes you need to decide how clients can instantiate them. As with the other framework design decisions, you need to balance generality, complexity, ease of learning, and ease of evolution in your choice of instantiation style. The four styles described here are no client instantiation, constructors, factory methods, and factory objects. These styles are not mutually exclusive. You may use more than one style for a given object or you may use different styles for different parts of the framework.

No Creation

The simplest and least powerful option is to prohibit clients from creating framework objects directly. The SWT event example cited above demonstrates this. By always constructing events inside the framework, the framework developers can guarantee that events are well formed. The framework code may be simpler if it can assume invariants about events.

The limitation of not allowing clients to create instances of framework classes is that it precludes legitimate uses of the classes the framework developer didn't anticipate. For very difficult programming tasks where any reduction of complexity would be welcome, eliminating the possibility of client-created objects may be a good choice. The value of a framework is often one not originally expected by the framework developers. Cutting off the chance for unexpected uses reduces the chance of finding additional valuable uses of the framework.

Constructors

Offering clients the ability to create objects through constructors is a simple option but one that creates substantial constraints on future change. When you publish a constructor, you are promising that the name of the class, the parameters required for creation, the package of the class, and (most constraining of all) the concrete class of the returned object won't change.

Most of the Java libraries offer creation through constructors. Once Sun published that lists are created by saying `new ArrayList()` they were committed to keeping a class named `ArrayList` in the `java.util` package without changing the concrete class returned. These are all substantial design constraints to maintain for the indefinite future, limiting the kind of changes Sun can make.

The advantage of representing object creation as a constructor is that it is simple and clear for clients. If clients need an easy-to-use creation interface and you don't mind giving up the ability to change the name, package, and concrete class of your abstractions, then constructors are a reasonable option.

Static Factories

Static factories add some complexity to object creation for clients but leave the framework developer more freedom for future design changes. If a client created a list by saying `ArrayList.create()` instead of using a constructor, then the name, package, and concrete class of the object returned could all be changed without affecting client code. A further step would be to concentrate the factory methods in a library class: `Collections.createArrayList()`. With this style of factory the only class that would need to remain in the original `java.util` package is the library class. All the other classes could move as necessary. On the other hand, the more abstract the creation, the harder it is to see where objects are created from reading the code.

Another advantage of factory methods is that they give you a chance to communicate clearly to clients the meaning of variations in construction. The purposes of two constructors with different sets of parameters are not always obvious, but the name of the factory methods can suggest the reason clients might want to create an object each way.

Factory Object

You can also represent instance creation by sending messages to a factory object instead of invoking a static method. For example, a `CollectionFactory` would provide methods for creating all the different kinds of collections. It might be used like this: `Collections.factory().createArrayList()`. A factory object provides even more flexibility than a static factory but is more complex to read. You need to trace the execution of code to see when certain classes are created.

As long as the factory is only accessed globally, a factory object doesn't provide any more flexibility than static factory methods. Factory objects show their power when they are used locally. For example, if you had special space-saving collections for use in mobile devices, you could initialize objects that needed to create collections with the space-saving collection factory if the code was running on a handset and a standard collection factory when running on a server.

Factory objects can be useful to create sets of classes that go together. If the Windows widgets work together but don't work with the Linux widgets, offering creation through a factory object is a way to help clients only create compatible classes.

Creation Conclusion

How you represent object creation in your framework affects how easy your framework is to use and change. One strategy is to offer factory methods for classes that are likely to change and constructors for stable classes. However, there is also value in a consistent creation strategy where all objects are created through factory methods or a factory object.

Methods

Other methods besides object creation also affect how easy it is to use and evolve your framework. The general strategy remains the same: reveal as few details as possible consistent with helping clients solve their problems.

Client-visible getters and setters are appropriate only when data structures are stable. Encouraging clients to rely on internal data structures dramatically reduces your options for future framework evolution. Setters are worse than getters in this regard. It is often possible to figure out an alternative way to compute a value that used to be stored in a field. Try to understand what problem the client is solving by setting a value. Rather than publish a setter, publish a method that is named for the problem the client needs to solve rather than the implementation.

For example, when writing a graphical widget library you might offer a Widget setter method setVisible(boolean). What happens when you introduce a third state, inactive? To simplify this for the client, publish intention-revealing methods like visible() and invisible(). These are what setVisible() means to the client. With these methods in place, adding inactive() to the superclass achieves the goal of not affecting client code.

Interface-based abstractions are slightly different. Adding inactive() to an interface breaks any client implementations of Widget. Instead, define an enumerated type States that records the possible widget states and publish a method setVisible(State). The variant with the boolean is an example of design information leaking out to clients. Booleans imply that there are only two possible states. The design with a single method and an enumerated type as a parameter allows the freedom to add other states should they become necessary.

This isn't to say that getters and setters should never be published for client use. If important framework functionality is implemented by returning or setting a field at the moment, publish the accessor. However, name the method so it doesn't reveal its implementation to clients.

Another method-level strategy for framework developers to maintain compatibility is to provide default values when you add parameters to published methods. If you add a parameter to a method, existing invocations of

CONCLUSION **129**

the method will need to be changed before client code will compile. However, you can keep client code working if you can keep the old method around and have it invoke the new method with a default parameter.

For example, suppose in JUnit you wanted the ability to pass a TestResult into a method that runs tests in classes. You could just modify the method by adding the parameter.

```
public TestResult run(Class... classes) {
  ....run tests in classes...
}
public void run(TestResult result, Class... classes) {
  ...run tests in classes...
}
```

Any client who invoked run(Class...) would have to change to add a TestResult parameter. However, the original method can supply a default parameter:

```
public TestResult run(Class... classes) {
  TestResult result= new TestResult();
  run(result, classes);
  return result;
}
```

By providing the default parameter, client code continues to work even though the interface also offers a new method.

Conclusion

Framework development and evolution requires some different implementation patterns than application development. The change to the economics of development from being dominated by the cost of understanding code to being dominated by the cost of upgrading client code calls for a substantial shift of both practices and values. For framework development, simplicity, the prime directive in application development, has lower priority than the need to remain free to further grow the framework. This is complicated when parts of an application are extracted to create a framework. Many of the application design decisions will need to be revisited to make an effective framework.

Frameworks evolve in a variety of ways. Sometimes the calculations of existing methods need improvement. Sometimes the calculations need to work with new kinds of parameters. Sometimes the framework can be used, with a little tweaking, to solve an entirely unexpected problem. Sometimes existing framework implementation details need to be published.

A metaphor that has served us well in JUnit is to look at a framework as the intersection of all the useful functionality in a domain rather than the union. It is the framework developer's job to ensure that clients can extend the framework to solve the remainder of their problems. It's tempting to try to solve a broad range of problems with a framework. The conflict is that the added functionality makes the framework that much more difficult to learn and use for all clients.

If every potential user of a framework has 90% of their requirements in common and 10% unique, then a framework to fully satisfy all developers will be much larger than a framework to satisfy only the common needs. As a framework developer it is my goal to meet the common needs of my users but not all their unique needs. If most users have to add the same functionality, then it belongs in the framework, but unique bits are best handled by the people with the direct need.

One way to encourage appropriately sized frameworks is to derive them from several concrete examples rather than starting from a general case. I wrote the precursor of JUnit after a half-dozen attempts to automatically test my code. Each variant solved only the problem I had right in front of me at the time. It was only from the perspective of having written the same code several times that I was able to see which problems were common to all tests and needed to be covered by the framework and which problems were unique to an individual situation.

Take the concepts in your framework from one or more clear and consistent metaphors. For example, if double-entry bookkeeping is the metaphor you use to record historical information, then clients will know to look for Account and Transaction. By choosing and applying metaphors consciously and communicating them to your clients, you make your frameworks easier to learn, use, and extend.

Deploying a framework does not need to be the end of evolution and growth. Care during the construction of the framework can result in a stable base for client applications and a dynamic foundation for further framework development.

Appendix A

Performance Measurement

This appendix describes the framework used to measure the data on collection performance described in Chapter 9. The problem is stated simply enough—accurately compare the time needed to perform several operations as they scale. However, the problem becomes more complicated when the accuracy of the timer is much less than the time required to complete the operations. The time tester presented here overcomes these problems by performing operations many times. It adapts to the accuracy of the timer by fixing the amount of wall clock time used to measure each operation.

Accurately benchmarking operations in an optimizing implementation of Java requires more knowledge than what is presented here, either in the framework or the tests themselves. To get accurate results, you need to know what the optimizer is likely to do with your code, to avoid the case where a clever implementation eliminates your operation completely. If the benchmark results don't match your intuition, that's an invitation to dig deeper. Either you will learn something about benchmarking or about the code you are measuring.

The code listed here is good enough to generate the data necessary for this book. It could be made more general. For example, the parameters for timing are represented as constants instead of as variables, there is no command line interface, and the reporting is simple and printed to the console. One important skill in programming is matching the effort to the return. Learning how to use patterns needs to be followed by learning when to use them and when to leave them in the bag.

Example

The timer should be able to measure operations written as simply as possible. Taking a cue from JUnit, operations to be tested are represented by methods. Instances of time tester methods will be constructed with a particular size so time tests can be made as data scales. For example, to test the time required to search a list, the test will look like this:

```
public class ListSearch {
  private List<Integer> numbers;
  private int probe;

  public ListSearch(int size) {
    numbers= new ArrayList<Integer>();
    for (int i= 0; i < size; i++)
      numbers.add(i);
    probe= size / 2;
  }

  public void search() {
    numbers.contains(probe);
  }
}
```

The result of running the framework with this class will be the time required to execute search() for collections of size 1, 10, 100, and so on.

API

The external interface for the timer is the class MethodsTimer. It is created with an array of methods:

```
public class MethodsTimer {
  private final Method[] methods;

  public MethodsTimer(Method[] methods) {
    this.methods= methods;
  }
}
```

Invoke a MethodsTimer by sending it report(). For example, to time the operations in ListSearch above, execute the following:

```
public static void main(String[] args) throws Exception {
  MethodsTimer tester= new MethodsTimer(ListSearch.class.getDeclaredMethods());
  tester.report();
}
```

Executing this method causes the results to be printed on the console:

```
search   34.89        130.61        989.73       9911.19       97410.83      990953.62
```

This means that the search operation takes 35 nanoseconds for a one-element list, 131 nanoseconds for a ten-element list, and so on.

The timer isn't perfectly accurate. Running it on the Nothing timer class times an empty method, which theoretically should result in all zeros. Instead, the answers (on my machine, anyway) are a few nanoseconds off:

```
nothing   1.92        -3.24        0.62        0.37        -0.74        2.30
```

Keep this accuracy in mind if you are timing very short operations. For example, to time array access I had to write a test method that accessed an array ten times to get accurate times. In general, though, a goal for the timer is for programmers to write simple operations and let the framework repeat the operations as many times as necessary to get an accurate time.

Implementation

Notice that the timer prints out six answers for each method that it times. This is because the timer is used to test operations as they scale. The report() method is a nested loop where the outer loop iterates through the methods to be timed and the inner loop iterates through sizes from 1, 10, . . ., 100,000.

```
private static final int MAXIMUM_SIZE= 100000;
public void report() throws Exception {
  for (Method each : methods) {
    System.out.print(each.getName() + "\t");
    for (int size= 1; size <= MAXIMUM_SIZE; size*= 10) {
      MethodTimer r= new MethodTimer(size, each);
      r.run();
      System.out.print(String.format("%.2f\t", r.getMethodTime()));
    }
    System.out.println();
  }
}
```

The reporting is as simple as possible, with tabs inserted between data elements so the data can easily be pasted into a spreadsheet. In a full-featured timer, I would probably compute all the MethodTimers first, then report them in a second step so the reporting could be more flexible.

MethodTimer

MethodsTimer relies on a helper object MethodTimer, a command which calculates the time required to execute a single method. The method will be invoked as many times as necessary until a sufficient amount of time has elapsed for an accurate reading. The time taken by the method, then, is the total divided by the number of invocations.

Each MethodTimer is constructed with a method and a size. Because the method may be invoked many times, each MethodTimer caches an object that can be sent a message invoking the method. It would take too long to create a new instance for every invocation. If an operation takes 50 nanoseconds, it will need to be executed 20,000,000 times to collect one second of data. Creating a 100,000-element list like the one used in ListSearch above takes ~50 milliseconds on my machine, so running this one test would take a week and a half. By caching the instance, the test takes only slightly longer than a second.

This reuse of instances is a different design from that of JUnit. In JUnit, a fresh instance is created for each test that is run. Tests are free to make changes to the instance's state, knowing that they are isolated from subsequent tests. The time tester provides no such freedom. Each timed method needs to leave the state of the test instance exactly as it found it.

Here is the MethodTimer constructor:

```
private final int size;
private final Method method;
private Object instance;

MethodTimer(int size, Method method) throws Exception {
  this.size= size;
  this.method= method;
  instance= createInstance();
}
```

Each method has a class, and it is that class that is instantiated when timing an operation. This implies that the current implementation does not support timing inherited methods, hence the call to getDeclaredMethods() in MethodsTimer. GetDeclaredMethods() only returns methods declared in the class, not superclasses. A more powerful design would be to annotate methods to be timed and search the whole superclass chain when looking for such methods. Hierarchies would eliminate some of the duplication you will see in the timers used for this book. (The specific timers used are later in this appendix.) Once again, this framework is only intended to be good enough for the purposes of this book. A framework used by many people requires a different design philosophy. Much greater investment is called for in a widely used framework, since any improvement enabled by a more powerful (if expensive) design is repaid a thousand times.

Creating the instance to be used involves finding a constructor that accepts an int as a parameter and invokes it.

```
private Object createInstance() throws Exception {
  Constructor<?> constructor= method.getDeclaringClass().getConstructor(new Class[]{int.class});
  return constructor.newInstance(new Object[]{size});
}
```

There are actually three factors required to compute the time necessary to run a single invocation of a method: the number of iterations, the total time to invoke the method that many times, and the overhead of invoking a method by reflection. Since method invocation by reflection can be expensive compared to the time required to execute the method (~150 nanoseconds on my machine), removing that overhead improves the accuracy of the timer. Each of these factors will be computed by the run() method and stored in fields.

```
private long totalTime;
private int iterations;
private long overhead;
double getMethodTime() {
  return (double) (totalTime - overhead) / (double) iterations;
}
```

The run() method is the heart of the timer. It invokes the method to be timed once, then twice, then four times, and so on until one second has been consumed. It then computes the overhead of however many dynamic invocations were required. After run() is finished, the MethodTimer is ready to be queried about its results. This temporal dependency between run() and any querying methods (like getMethodTime() above) is a bit ugly. The alternative is to have the constructor also compute the run-time. I'm reluctant to have constructors do significant work, because I like having the freedom to decouple creating the instances from doing the work. Designed this way, I can, if I choose, create a collection of MethodTimers and pass them around, serialize them, or send them over a network, without worrying about performance.

```
void run() throws Exception {
  iterations= 1;
  while (true) {
    totalTime= computeTotalTime();
    if (totalTime > MethodsTimer.ONE_SECOND)
      break;
    iterations*= 2;
  }
  overhead= overheadTimer(iterations).computeTotalTime();
}
```

Notice the use of another constant, ONE_SECOND, in MethodsTimer. Using constants for configuration is a low-cost way of providing some flexibility for users who are willing to edit the source code, but such constants are best put together in one place so they are easy to find.

```
static final int ONE_SECOND= 1000000000;
```

Canceling Overhead

All that is left of the framework is the methods for computing the dynamic method invocation overhead. The static factory method overheadTimer() is intended to communicate the purpose of this special timer.

It is a little strange to have one MethodTimer invoke another as part of its work, but after several experiments this was the best way I found to structure the code.

```
private static MethodTimer overheadTimer(int iterations) throws Exception {
  return new MethodTimer(iterations);
}

private MethodTimer(int iterations) throws Exception {
  this(0, MethodTimer.Overhead.class.getMethod("nothing", new Class[0]));
  this.iterations= iterations;
}

public static class Overhead {
  public Overhead(int size) {
  }

  public void nothing() {
  }
}
```

Tests

Here are the tests used to generate the data presented in the chapter "Collections." They demonstrate the use of the timer framework, some of the peculiarities of the collection classes, and at the same time some of the limitation of the design presented here.

Comparing Collections

The first example compares using a Set and an ArrayList as a Collection. The constructor creates the two collections of the given size and initializes them. The data used as elements are strings. The hash values of the strings will not be randomly distributed. However, I tried using Integers as the data and found that the behavior was even stranger. Since hash values for large sets are seldom randomly distributed, if large-scale performance matters to you, you may wish to create "typical" data representing the elements you compute with if you are timing collections for your own use.

Each set of timing tests is represented as a class. The timings themselves are represented by the methods of that class. The class stores the collections to be computed with. Note that both are declared as Collection. The class also stores a probe, which is an element to be searched for later.

```
public class SetVsArrayList {
  private Collection<String> set;
  private Collection<String> arrayList;
  private String probe;
}
```

To initialize an instance, the collections are filled with elements. Notice that the probe is in the middle of the collection, so as to provide a "worst case" scenario. A more thorough examination of collection performance would use elements from the beginning, middle, and end of the collection.

```
public SetVsArrayList(int size) {
  set= new HashSet<String>(size);
  arrayList= new ArrayList<String>(size);
  for (int i= 0; i < size; i++) {
    String element= String.format("a%d", i);
    set.add(element);
    arrayList.add(element);
  }
  probe= String.format("a%d", size / 2);
}
```

The first pair of operations compares the time required to test for set membership. The only difference between the two methods is the collection tested. The time required for HashSet membership is nearly constant, while the time required for ArrayList membership grows linearly with the size of the collection.

```
public void setMembership() {
  set.contains(probe);
}
```

```
public void arrayListMembership() {
  arrayList.contains(probe);
}
```

The duplication between these methods suggests an alternative API with less duplication, where the test class would contain an abstract implementation of the methods to be timed. Each instance would be initialized with the concrete class to be tested:

```
public class CollectionOperations {
  Collection<String> collection;
  String probe;
  public void membership() {
    collection.contains(probe);
  }
}b
```

The concrete collection class could be initialized either in a constructor or in a subclass. While this design results in less duplication and would be superior for a widely distributed framework, the current design is good enough for the data needed for this book, and so I will leave in the duplication.

Another pair of methods in SetVsArrayList measures the time required to iterate over the collections. The time required is linear in the number of elements.

```
public void setIteration() {
  Iterator<String> all= set.iterator();
  while (all.hasNext())
    all.next();
}
```

```
public void arrayListIteration() {
  Iterator<String> all= arrayList.iterator();
  while (all.hasNext())
    all.next();
}
```

I tried profiling iteration with a for loop, for (String each : set);, but the Java implementation was clever enough to notice the null loop body and eliminate the loop entirely. In general, one of the challenges of writing timing methods is keeping the methods simple while not allowing Java's optimizations to eliminate the method entirely. Always check your results to be sure they make sense. If not, try another way to express the same calculation.

The final timing methods check the time required to modify a collection. The methods are careful to leave the collections unchanged as a result. This is a limitation of the timing framework: since each method will be invoked many times with the same object, the methods need to leave the state of the object unchanged.

```
public void setModification() {
  set.add("b");
  set.remove("b");
}

public void arrayListModification() {
  arrayList.add("b");
  arrayList.remove("b");
}
```

The timings of these operations are the same as the timing of membership testing: HashSet is roughly constant and ArrayList is linear.

Comparing ArrayList and LinkedList

This test is similar to the test above, except that the variables to be tested are declared as List instead of Collection, and are initialized to an ArrayList and a LinkedList.

```
public class Lists {

  private List<String> arrayList;
  private List<String> linkedList;
  private final int size;
}
```

Rather than store an element to probe for, as was done when testing collections, this test remembers the size of the collections to be used later with List's get(int) method.

```
public Lists(int size) {
  this.size= size;
  arrayList= new ArrayList<String>(size);
  linkedList= new LinkedList<String>();
  for (int i= 0; i < size; i++) {
    String element= String.format("a%d", i);
    arrayList.add(element);
    linkedList.add(element);
  }
}
```

The first pair of tests measures the time required to modify a collection by inserting and then removing an element. Notice that the element is inserted at the beginning of the collection. ArrayList optimizes insertion at the end so that it takes constant time, just like LinkedList, instead of linear time.

```
public void arrayListModification() {
  arrayList.add(0, "b");
  arrayList.remove(0);
}
```

```
public void linkedListModification() {
  linkedList.add(0, "b");
  linkedList.remove(0);
}
```

The other test measures the time required to access an element. The results are the mirror of the modification test: ArrayList access is constant time and LinkedList access is linear. My first version of this test accessed the element at the end of the collection, but LinkedList turns out to optimize this case by searching backwards from the end for indices greater than half of their size.

```
public void arrayListAccess() {
  arrayList.get(size / 2);
}
```

```
public void linkedListAccess() {
  linkedList.get(size / 2);
}
```

Comparing Sets

Sets follow the same basic pattern used in comparing lists above. The two operations compared are modification and membership, since most other operations are either built from these operations or display a similar performance profile. In the code below, I will only show one variant of each of the timing methods since the other variants are identical except for the set to which the messages are sent.

The three set implementations compared are HashSet, LinkedHashSet, and TreeSet. Properly speaking, TreeSet is an implementation of SortedSet, but I thought it would be useful to compare the overhead imposed by keeping the elements in sorted order.

```
public class Sets {
  private Set<String> hashSet;
  private Set<String> linkedHashSet;
  private Set<String> treeSet;
  private String probe;
}
```

The constructor initializes each of the sets with identical elements and initializes a probe to be used later in timing membership. Notice that each set is created with the capacity to store the appropriate number of elements. All the Java literature I've read stresses the importance of pre-allocating the right size of collections. However, my measurements show that pre-allocating zero elements is within 10% of pre-allocating the final number of elements.

```
public Sets(int size) {
  hashSet= new HashSet<String>(size);
  linkedHashSet= new LinkedHashSet<String>(size);
  treeSet= new TreeSet<String>();
  for (int i= 0; i < size; i++) {
    String element= String.format("a%d", i);
    hashSet.add(element);
    linkedHashSet.add(element);
    treeSet.add(element);
  }
  probe= String.format("a%d", size / 2);
}
```

To time membership, search the set for the pre-computed probe. The other set implementations are timed similarly.

```
public void hashSetContains() {
  hashSet.contains(probe);
}
```

The modification timing method adds and then removes the same element, leaving the set unchanged.

```
public void hashSetModification() {
  hashSet.add("b");
  hashSet.remove("b");
}
```

Comparing Maps

Timing maps is much the same as timing sets. Again, there are three implementations available from the Java library—HashMap, LinkedHashMap, and TreeMap. The timing results are the same, since the sets are implemented as maps. That is, a HashSet uses a HashMap internally to store the elements, and so on.

```
public class Maps {
  private Map<String, String> hashMap;
  private Map<String, String> linkedHashMap;
  private Map<String, String> treeMap;
  private String probe;
```

Initializing the maps requires sending them put() instead of add(). I chose to have the key and value the same, since it doesn't matter for timing purposes what the values are.

```
public Maps(int size) {
  hashMap= new HashMap<String, String>(size);
  linkedHashMap= new LinkedHashMap<String, String>(size);
  treeMap= new TreeMap<String, String>();
  for (int i= 0; i < size; i++) {
    String element= String.format("a%d", i);
    hashMap.put(element, element);
    linkedHashMap.put(element, element);
    treeMap.put(element, element);
  }
  probe= String.format("a%d", size / 2);
}
```

The two timing methods use the map operations containsKey() and put() instead of the set operations contains() and add(). Other than that they are identical.

```
public void hashMapContains() {
  hashMap.containsKey(probe);
}
public void hashMapModification() {
  hashMap.put("b", "b");
  hashMap.remove("b");
}
```

Conclusion

The framework and examples above offer lessons at several levels. One is the value of getting data. Widely held beliefs like "pre-allocating sets improves performance" deserve careful scrutiny. Before adding complexity to a program, be sure the complexity brings benefits. Sometimes the only way to find out if the benefits accrue is to go and measure them.

Another lesson in the methods timer framework is the importance of adjusting coding style based on context. I would have designed and coded the framework very differently if I had a larger audience or more timing tests to write. As it was, the simplifying assumptions I made reduced the total effort of writing the framework and tests. Dogmatic advice like "Always include all flexibility you can imagine" or "code for today, forget about tomorrow" is equally wrongheaded.

Finally, the code in this chapter offers examples of many of the implementation patterns in the rest of the book. Complete Constructors, Intention-Revealing Names, and so on are represented in every line of code. Whether they served to communicate my intentions or not is something only you can judge. If not, figure out patterns for yourself that would better serve to communicate. In the end, this is the big lesson of this book: that a programmer's job is to communicate with other programmers, not just a machine. Programming, then, is a human task done by humans for humans. It doesn't need to be an escape from society. It can be a means of connecting. Oh, and writing good code at the same time.

Bibliography

Here is a list of books that I have found helpful as I learn to program.

General Programming

Kent Beck, *Smalltalk Best Practice Patterns*, Prentice Hall, 1997. ISBN 013476904X.
> The implementation patterns for Smalltalk. Many are similar to the patterns listed here, but there are also significant differences because the languages are so different. Writing it forced me to slow down and think through decisions that I had been making on instinct.

Martin Fowler, *Refactoring: Improving the Design of Existing Code*, Addison-Wesley, 1999. ISBN 0201485672.
> It is easy to say that designs should change a little at a time. This book introduced how to make those changes.

Eric Freeman and Elisabeth Freeman, *Head First Design Patterns*, O'Reilly Media, 2004. ISBN 0596007124.
> An alternative, visually-oriented introduction to design patterns.

Erich Gamma, Richard Helm, Ralph Johnson, and John Vlissides, *Design Patterns: Elements of Reusable Object-Oriented Software*, Addison-Wesley, 1995. ISBN 0201633612.
> The classic description of large-scale repeating structures in code.

Daniel Hoffman and David Weiss, *Software Fundamentals: Collected Papers by David L. Parnas*, Addison-Wesley, 2001. ISBN 0201703696.
> Describes the theoretical underpinnings of good software.

Andrew Hunt and David Thomas, *The Pragmatic Programmer*, Addison-Wesley, 2000. ISBN 020161622X.

    The attitude of a professional programmer is clear from this book: curious, honest, always learning.

Brian Kernighan and Rob Pike, *The Practice of Programming*, Addison-Wesley, 1999. ISBN 020161586X.

    Another demonstration of thoroughly professional programmers at work.

Donald Knuth, *The Art of Computer Programming: Volume 1, Fundamental Algorithms, 3rd Edition*, Addison-Wesley, 1997. ISBN 0201896834.

Donald Knuth, *The Art of Computer Programming: Volume 2, Seminumerical Algorithms, 3rd Edition*, Addison-Wesley, 1997. ISBN 0201896842.

Donald Knuth, *The Art of Computer Programming: Volume 3, Searching and Sorting, 2nd Edition*, Addison-Wesley, 1998. ISBN 0201896850.

    Professor Knuth clearly loves programming and conveys his love through his writing.

Donald Knuth, *Literate Programming*, Center for the Study of Language and Information, 1992. ISBN 0937073806.

    One of the first books to focus on the need for programmers to communicate with other programmers. Source of one of my favorite quotes, "A program should read like a book." It's not always worthwhile to go as far as a literate program, but the attitude is right on.

Steve McConnell, *Code Complete: A Practical Handbook of Software Construction, 2nd Edition*, Microsoft Press, 2004. ISBN 0735619670.

    Surveys the techniques required to program responsibly.

Diomidis Spinellis, *Code Reading*, Addison-Wesley, 2003. ISBN 0201799405.

    A view from the other side: how to read code. *Code Reading* is *Implementation Patterns'* mirror image, reading for understanding as contrasted with writing for understanding.

Edward Yourdon, *Techniques of Program Structure and Design*, Prentice Hall, 1975. ISBN 013901702X.

    One of the earliest explanations of what makes a good program. The principles are still sound even if the examples seem dated.

Edward Yourdon and Larry Constantine, *Structured Design: Fundamentals of a Discipline of Computer Program and Systems Design*, Prentice Hall, 1979. ISBN 0138544719.

    This book presents the equivalent of the laws of physics for software design and grounds the discussion on the economics of development.

Philosophy

Christopher Alexander, *Notes on the Synthesis of Form*, Harvard University Press, 1964. ISBN 0674627512.
> Explains the theory behind patterns: recurring decisions with recurring patterns of constraints and similar solutions.

Christopher Alexander, *The Timeless Way of Building*, Oxford University Press, 1979. ISBN 0195024028.
> The theoretical description of design and construction with patterns. A common theme is the advantages of designing a little at a time using feedback from earlier design, construction, and use.

Christopher Alexander, Sara Ishikawa, Murray Silverstein with Max Jacobson, Ingrid Fiksdahl-King, Shlomo Angel, *A Pattern Language*, Oxford University Press, 1977. ISBN 0195019199.
> An example of a wide-ranging pattern language. Also useful when designing workspaces and houses.

Richard Gabriel, *Patterns of Software*, Oxford University Press, 1996. ISBN 019510269X.
> A collection of essays about applying pattern-style thinking to software development.

Robert Grudin, *The Grace of Great Things*, Ticknor and Fields, 1990. ISBN 0395588685.
> Celebrates and encourages exceptionally good design.

Leonard Koren, *Wabi-Sabi for Artists, Designers, Poets, and Philosophers*, Stone Bridge Press, 1994. ISBN 1880656124.
> Effective design isn't a search for perfection but of sufficiency. Wabi-sabi is a Japanese aesthetic of real beauty, sometimes rough but always functional.

D'Arcy Thompson, *On Growth and Form*, Cambridge University Press, 1961. ISBN 0521437768.
> An often-difficult book about the way complexity is created and expressed in the natural world.

Edward Tufte, *The Visual Display of Quantitative Information*, Graphics Press, 1983. ISBN 0961392142.
> An engaging example of principle-based thinking, in this case about graphic design.

Java

Joshua Bloch, *Effective Java Programming Language Guide*, Addison-Wesley, 2001. ISBN 0201310058.

An early description of how to use Java including a fair amount of implicit information about why Java is the way it is.

Bruce Eckel, *Thinking in Java, 4th Edition*, Prentice Hall, 2006. ISBN 0131872486.

My Java bible. When I need to know how something works in Java, this is the book I open.

Steven Metsker, *Design Patterns Java Workbook*, Addison-Wesley, 2002. ISBN 0201743973.

Shows how Java affects the general design patterns.

Index

MORE FROM THE FOUNDER OF EXTREME PROGRAMMING

Don't miss these classic texts from Kent Beck, one of the software industry's most creative and acclaimed leaders, who passionately employs patterns, extreme programming, and test-driven development.

ISBN 9780321146533

By driving development with automated tests and then eliminating duplication, any developer can write reliable, bug-free code no matter the level of complexity. Kent Beck reveals the power of test-driven development with this book, which follows TDD projects from start to finish, illustrating techniques programmers can use to easily and dramatically increase the quality of their work.

ISBN 9780321278654

"The first edition of this book told us what XP was—it changed the way many of us think about software development. This second edition takes it farther and gives us a lot more of the 'whys' of XP, the motivations and the principles behind the practices. This is great stuff."

—Dave Thomas, The Pragmatic Programmers LLC

THIS BOOK IS SAFARI ENABLED

INCLUDES FREE 45-DAY ACCESS TO THE ONLINE EDITION

The Safari® Enabled icon on the cover of your favorite technology book means the book is available through Safari Bookshelf. When you buy this book, you get free access to the online edition for 45 days.

Safari Bookshelf is an electronic reference library that lets you easily search thousands of technical books, find code samples, download chapters, and access technical information whenever and wherever you need it.

TO GAIN 45-DAY SAFARI ENABLED ACCESS TO THIS BOOK:

- Go to **http://www.awprofessional.com/safarienabled**

- Complete the brief registration form

- Enter the coupon code found in the front of this book on the "Copyright" page

Addison
Wesley

If you have difficulty registering on Safari Bookshelf or accessing the online edition, please e-mail customer-service@safaribooksonline.com.

Register
Your Book

at www.informit.com/register

You may be eligible to receive:

- Advance notice of forthcoming editions of the book
- Related book recommendations
- Chapter excerpts and supplements of forthcoming titles
- Information about special contests and promotions throughout the year
- Notices and reminders about author appearances, tradeshows, and online chats with special guests

Contact us

If you are interested in writing a book or reviewing manuscripts prior to publication, please write to us at:

Editorial Department
Addison-Wesley Professional
75 Arlington Street, Suite 300
Boston, MA 02116 USA
Email: AWPro@aw.com

Visit us on the Web: http://www.awprofessional.com